Government of
**Western
Australia**

# STATE LIBRARY OF
# WESTERN AUSTRALIA

✓ **W9-BEU-483**

**This item is due for return on or before the last date stamped below.
Items will be renewed or reserved on application unless required by another reader.**

This item was purchased by the State Government of Western Australia and managed by the State Library of Western Australia for the WA public library network. You have access to over 2 million items throughout the network.

Items of interest found on our catalogue at
## http://www.slwa.wa.gov.au
can be requested through your local public library.

**Your Guide to Knowledge**

LB 0014L

# The Modern Wit

Shelley Klein

Michael O'Mara Books Limited

First published in Great Britain in 2008 by
Michael O'Mara Books Limited
9 Lion Yard
Tremadoc Road
London SW4 7NQ

A CIP catalogue record for this book is available from the
British Library.

Papers used by Michael O'Mara Books Limited are natural,
recyclable products made from wood grown in sustainable
forests. The manufacturing processes conform to the
environmental regulations of the country of origin.

ISBN: 978-1-84317-254-3

1 3 5 7 9 10 8 6 4 2

www.mombooks.com

Typeset by K.DESIGN, Winscombe, Somerset
Printed and bound in Great Britain by
Cox & Wyman, Reading, Berks

# CONTENTS

'No comment, but don't quote me.'
DAN QUAYLE

# INTRODUCTION

'The surest way of making a monkey out of a man is to quote him,' wrote Robert Benchley. But, if this compendium of modern wit reveals anything, it is that the people who are quoted on its pages are as far from monkeys as you could hope to get. Instead, the likes of Woody Allen, Victoria Wood, Bill Hicks, Stephen Fry, Jay Leno and Dawn French add up to not only the funniest men and women around, but also the cleverest. In their individual styles and distinctly witty ways they have all taken a great deal of time and care to comment on the world around them and report back to us with comic panache.

Take, for example, Joan Rivers's comment on going to see a Jewish porn film, ' . . . one minute of sex and nine minutes of guilt,' or Billy Connolly's observation that, 'Marriage is a wonderful invention; but, then again, so is a bicycle repair kit.' Indeed, this collection, comprising the best comic utterances from the last thirty years or so, covers the widest variety of subject matter possible – from sex to sexism, politics to the politically incorrect, God and godlessness, xenophobia, old age, the film industry and death. Of course, some of the commentators take their observations a lot further than others; thus, the section entitled 'How Very Insulting' contains some of the most cutting remarks in the book, such as Boy George's dig that, 'Prince looks like a dwarf who's been dipped in a bucket of pubic hair,' or Gore Vidal's quip that Ronald Reagan was, 'A triumph of the embalmer's art.'

Politics is also high on the list of most-quoted-upon subjects, with many of today's foremost writers and broadcasters (Matthew Parris, David Letterman, Jay Leno, etc.)

taking particular pleasure in sticking the knife into those in power. Unsurprisingly, however, the most popular subject of all – and one that will be found in any dictionary of quotations, however old or out-of-date – is, and probably always will be, sex. Sex is manna from heaven for anyone wishing to make a funny joke or a scathing remark, like actor and general funny man Steve Martin's quip that 'Sex is one of the most beautiful, wholesome and natural things that money can buy,' or columnist Christopher Hitchens's comment that 'The four most overrated things in life are champagne, lobster, anal sex and picnics.' In fact, sex brings out the best (or worst, depending on your point of view) in almost everyone, from Woody Allen ('Hey, don't knock masturbation! It's sex with someone I love') to Zsa Zsa Gabor ('Personally I know nothing about sex because I've always been married'). No doubt because it's a fact of life and something almost everyone does, sex is universal fodder for the greatest wisecracks, tickling the fancy the whole world over.

Another equally hilarious topic and one that is close to the heart of most women is the subject of men. Famously (or should that be infamously?), Roseanne Barr is the progenitor of some of the most scathing remarks about the hairier sex, such as, 'Men can read maps better than women. 'Cause only the male mind could conceive of one inch equalling a hundred miles.' But not to be outdone by the women, there are plenty of none-too-flattering remarks made by the men (particularly in the category entitled 'Sexual Politics') about wives, mothers and girlfriends. In fact, when it comes to modern humour, there are very few sections of society that escape observation. No subject is off-limits, no celebrity is safe, and no nationality is above being lampooned.

Indeed, in this collection, sex, death, old age, television, the nuclear family and infancy all come under the comic microscope. I have also endeavoured to include most of the big comedic names from both sides of the Atlantic, such as John Cleese, Bill Cosby, Billy Connolly, Eddie Izzard, Robin Williams, Joan Rivers, Harry Hill, Steve Martin, Spike Milligan, Alan Bennett, P. J. O'Rourke, Stephen Fry and Homer Simpson . . . to name but a few. From the sublime to the ridiculous, from the surreal to the plain dumb, you should be able to find every type of humour catered for in *The Modern Wit*. So, as Eric Idle says in *The Life of Brian*, 'Always look on the bright side of life' because, with this book by your bedside table, you'll never be short of a laugh.

Shelley Klein, 2007

# MEN

When I eventually met Mr Right I had no idea
that his first name was Always.

**RITA RUDNER**

**❋**

Women might be able to fake orgasms.
But men can fake whole relationships.

**SHARON STONE**

**❋**

I don't hate men. I think men are absolutely
fantastic . . . as a concept.

**JO BRAND**

**❋**

The problem with men is they are arseholes. The problem
with women is that they put up with these arseholes.

**CHER**

**❋**

I love men even though they're lying, cheating scumbags.

**GWYNETH PALTROW**

**❋**

Macho does not prove mucho.

**ZSA ZSA GABOR**

**❋**

It's no news to anyone that nice guys finish last.
Almost every female I know has had the uncomfortable
experience of going out with a 'nice man'. Spelled 'N-E-R-D'.
How many times has your girlfriend said, 'He's so sweet
and so cute, so why don't I like him?' Let's face it, when an
attractive but ALOOF ('cool') man comes along, there are
some of us who offer to shine his shoes with our underpants.
If he has a mean streak, somehow this is 'attractive'. There
are thousands of scientific concepts as to why this is so,
and yes, yes, it's very sick – but none of this helps.

LYNDA BARRY, *BIG IDEAS*, CARTOON, 1983

■■

A good man doesn't just happen. They have to be
created by us women. A guy is a lump, like a doughnut.
So first you gotta get rid of all the stuff his mom did to
him. And then you gotta get rid of all that macho crap
they pick up from beer commercials. And then there's
my personal favourite, the male ego.

ROSEANNE BARR

■■

The man has not been born for whom
I will iron a shirt.

KATE O'MARA

■■

Men should be like Kleenex – soft, strong and disposable.

CHER

■■

Men do not like to admit even momentary imperfection.
My husband forgot the code to turn off the alarm.
When the police came, he wouldn't admit he'd forgotten
the code . . . he turned himself in.

RITA RUDNER

■■

Women were brought up to believe that men
were the answer. They weren't. They weren't
even one of the questions.

JULIAN BARNES

■■

They say men can never experience the pain of childbirth.
They can . . . if you hit them in the goolies with a cricket
bat for fourteen hours.

JO BRAND

■■

A man is designed to walk three miles in the rain to
phone for help when the car breaks down – and a
woman is designed to say, 'You took your time' when
he comes back dripping wet.

VICTORIA WOOD

■■

Men can read maps better than women. 'Cause only the male
mind could conceive of one inch equalling a hundred miles.

ROSEANNE BARR

■■

. . . Why is commitment such a big problem for a man?
When a man is driving down that freeway of love, the
woman he's with is like an exit, but he doesn't want to get off
there. He wants to keep driving. And the woman is like,
'Look, gas, food, lodging, that's our exit, that's everything we
need to be happy . . . Get off here, now!' But the man is
focusing on the sign underneath that says, 'Next exit 27
miles,' and he thinks, 'I can make it!' Sometimes he can,
sometimes he can't. Sometimes, the car ends up on the side
of the road, hood up and smoke pouring out of the engine.
He's sitting on the kerb all alone, thinking 'I guess
I didn't realize how many miles I was racking up.'

**JERRY SEINFELD**

There are three stages of man: he believes in Santa Claus;
he doesn't believe in Santa Claus; he is Santa Claus.

**BOB PHILLIPS**

The male is a domestic animal which, if treated with
firmness and kindness, can be trained to do most things.

**JILLY COOPER**

How do you know if it's time to wash the dishes
and clean your house? Look inside your pants.
If you find a penis in there, it's not time.

**JO BRAND**

# SEX MAD

Is sex dirty? Only if it's done right.

**WOODY ALLEN, *EVERYTHING YOU ALWAYS WANTED TO KNOW ABOUT SEX BUT WERE AFRAID TO ASK***

∷

Sex is the biggest nothing of all time.

**ANDY WARHOL**

∷

If the Nobel Prize was awarded by a woman, it would go to the inventor of the dimmer switch. This is the greatest sex aid known to womankind. Well, to women over a certain age, say sixteen.

**KATHY LETTE, *ALTAR EGO***

∷

I practice safe sex – I use an airbag.

**GARRY SHANDLING**

∷

Lady Rumpers: And then you took me.
Sir Percy: I took *you*? You took *me*. Your Land Army breeches came down with a fluency born of long practice.

**ALAN BENNETT, *HABEAS CORPUS***

∷

There's a sexual revolution going on, and I think that
with our current foreign policy, we'll probably be sending
troops in there any minute to break it up.

**MEL BROOKS**

Sometimes I got so bored of trying to touch her breasts
that I would try to touch her between the legs, a gesture
that had a sort of self-parodying wit about it: it was like
trying to borrow a fiver, getting turned down and asking
to borrow fifty quid.

**NICK HORNBY, *HIGH FIDELITY***

For flavour, Instant Sex will never supersede the
stuff you had to peel and cook.

**QUENTIN CRISP**

There's a new medical crisis. Doctors are reporting that
many men are having allergic reactions to latex condoms.
They say they cause severe swelling. So what's the problem?

**DUSTIN HOFFMAN**

Every day is President's Day when you have an intern!

**DAVID LETTERMAN**

I can spot an ex-public schoolboy from a mile off.
Bum, bum and buggery.

HUGH GRANT, QUOTED IN RICHARD E. GRANT'S *WITH NAILS*

■■

Aprons are sexy, with or without clothes on underneath.
We all fantasize about a man in a pinny . . .

CATHERINE ZETA-JONES

■■

Part of the fun was the thought that there John Major
was sitting in the Whips' Office, sometimes discussing
other people's affairs, and keeping very quiet about
his own. I loved that feeling.

EDWINA CURRIE, *DIARIES 1987–1992*

■■

Swans mate for life, and look how bad-tempered they are.

JEFF GREEN

■■

The big difference between sex for money and sex for
free is that sex for money usually costs less.

BRENDAN FRANCIS

■■

Hey, don't knock masturbation! It's sex with someone I love.

WOODY ALLEN, *ANNIE HALL*

■■

Woke up having sex – with a terrible hangover.

TRACEY EMIN, *STRANGELAND*

**::**

Sex is one of the most beautiful, wholesome and
natural things that money can buy.

STEVE MARTIN

**::**

I never knew there *was* a local sex shop and I still
don't know where it is – not, I'd like to make it clear,
that I've searched for it.

SIMON GRAY, *FAT CHANCE*

**::**

I never miss a chance to have sex or appear on television.

GORE VIDAL

**::**

A fast word about oral contraception. I asked a girl
to go to bed with me and she said 'No.'

WOODY ALLEN

**::**

My ultimate fantasy is to entice a man to my bedroom,
put a gun to his head, and say, 'Make babies or die.'

RUBY WAX

**::**

I saw my first porno film recently – a Jewish porno film – one minute of sex and nine minutes of guilt.

**JOAN RIVERS**

I like my coffee like I like my women – in a plastic cup.

**EDDIE IZZARD**

Foreplay is like beefburgers – three minutes each side.

**VICTORIA WOOD**

Seems to me the basic conflict between men and women, sexually, is that men are like firemen. To men, sex is an emergency, and no matter what we're doing we can be ready in two minutes. Women, on the other hand, are like fire. They're very exciting, but the conditions have to be exactly right for it to occur.

**JERRY SEINFELD**

The four most overrated things in life are champagne, lobster, anal sex and picnics.

**CHRISTOPHER HITCHENS**

I was with this girl the other night and from the way she was responding to my skilful caresses, you would have sworn she was conscious from the top of her head to the tag on her toes.

**EMO PHILIPS**

▓

Austin Powers: How do you get into those pants?
Felicity Shagwell: Well, you can start by buying me a drink.

**MIKE MYERS, *AUSTIN POWERS: THE SPY WHO SHAGGED ME***

▓

My mother used to say, 'Delia, if S-E-X ever rears its ugly head, close your eyes before you see the rest of it.'

**ALAN AYCKBOURN, *THE BEDROOM FARCE***

▓

Zeus performed acts with swans and heifers that would debar him from every London club except the Garrick or possibly the Naval and Military.

**STEPHEN FRY**

▓

Women are removing sperm from the bodies of their dead husbands. Kind of ironic. When they're alive, most men can't give it away.

**JAY LENO**

▓

Sex without using someone is as difficult
as eating without chewing.

JULIE BURCHILL

. . . men generally pay for all expenses on a date . . .
Either sex, however, may bring a little gift, its value
to be determined by the bizarreness of the sexual
request to be made later that evening.

P. J. O'ROURKE, *MODERN MANNERS*

With the casino and the beds, our passengers will have
at least two ways to get lucky on one of our flights.

RICHARD BRANSON

We all know girls do it. But if you ask them to do it,
they say no. Why? Because they want to be proper.
Finally, after thirteen years of courtship and dates
and so on, one night they get drunk and they do it.
And after they've done it, that's all they want to do.
Now they're fallen, now they're disgraced, and all
they want is to do it. You say, 'Let's have a cup of tea.'
No, let's do it. 'Let's go to the cinema.'
No, I'd rather do it.

MEL BROOKS

Most men approach sex a lot like shooting a game of pinball. We don't have any idea about the internal workings or what we should do to win, we're just gonna try to keep the ball in play as long as possible.

**TIM STEEVES**

❄

Sex is the most beautiful thing that can take place between a happily married man and his secretary.

**BARRY HUMPHRIES**

❄

I'm not a social person, but I could fall for a duke – they are a great aphrodisiac.

**TINA BROWN**

❄

The fact is I am not having sex. But I feel absolutely ripe for the – what would you say – plucking?

**ANGELINA JOLIE**

❄

My love life is terrible. The last time I was inside a woman was when I visited the Statue of Liberty.

**WOODY ALLEN, *CRIMES AND MISDEMEANORS***

❄

# FOOD AND DRINK

The menu is a triumph of invention that manages to offer *everything* cholesterol-free, dairy-free, preservative-free and sugar-free at a GREAT FEE.

RICHARD E. GRANT, *WITH NAILS*

∷

Edmund Blackadder: If you were to serve up one of your meals in Staff HQ, you would be arrested for the greatest mass poisoning since Lucretia Borgia invited 500 of her close friends round for a wine and anthrax party.

RICHARD CURTIS AND BEN ELTON, WRITERS, *BLACKADDER*

∷

We were meant to eat meat. We have fangs in our mouth. Everything with fangs eats meat. When was the last time you saw a lion stalking rhubarb?

HARLAND WILLIAMS

∷

That's not an act of love. It's an act of hate.

RAYMOND BLANC ON ENGLISH FOOD

∷

I went to a restaurant that serves 'breakfast at any time'.
So I ordered French Toast during the Renaissance.

**STEVEN WRIGHT**

■■

I think Pringles' intention was to make tennis balls.
But the day the rubber was supposed to show up,
they got a big load of potatoes instead.

**MITCH HEDBERG**

■■

I never do any television without chocolate. That's my motto
and I live by it. Quite often I write the scripts and I make
sure there are chocolate scenes. Actually I'm a bit of a
chocolate tart and will eat anything. It's amazing I'm so slim.

**DAWN FRENCH**

■■

I can never understand why they cook on TV. I can't smell it.
Can't eat it. Can't taste it. At the end of the show they
hold it up to the camera. 'Well, here it is. You can't have any.
Thanks for watching. Goodbye.'

**JERRY SEINFELD**

■■

Why does mineral water that 'has trickled through
mountains for centuries' have a use-by date?

**PETER KAY**

■■

The worst thing that ever happened to me was that I offered a fellow a crisp from my bag and he took two.

VIC REEVES

##

Mrs Doyle: Are you looking forward to your lunch tomorrow, Father?
Ted: Hmmm? I suppose so.
Mrs Doyle: You do like pheasant, don't you, Father?
Ted: Pheasant? I *love* pheasant.
Mrs Doyle: Well, there's a little clue. The thing you'll be eating likes pheasant as well.

ARTHUR MATHEWS AND GRAHAM LINEHAN,
WRITERS, *FATHER TED*

##

I went into a McDonald's yesterday and said, 'I'd like some fries.' The girl at the counter said, 'Would you like some fries with that?'

JAY LENO

##

The most remarkable thing about my mother is that for thirty years she served nothing but leftovers. The original meal was never found.

TRACEY ULLMAN

##

For years I was an undiagnosed anorexic, suffering from a little-known variant of the disease, where, freakishly, the appetite turns in on itself and demands more and more food, forcing the sufferer to gain several stones in weight and wear men's V-necked pullovers. My condition has stabilized now, but I can never stray too far from cocoa-based products and I keep a small cracknel-type candy in my brassiere at all times. Fortunately I wear a D-cup, so there is plenty of room for sweetmeats . . .

VICTORIA WOOD

You can eat a man, but I'm not sure of the fibre content.

JENNY ECLAIR

There are two kinds of women in this world – those who love chocolate and complete bitches.

DAWN FRENCH

I can't bear salad. It grows while you're eating it, you know. Have you noticed? You start one side of your plate and by the time you've got to the other, there's a fresh crop of lettuce taken root and sprouted up.

ALAN AYCKBOURN, *LIVING TOGETHER*

Life is too short to stuff a mushroom.

SHIRLEY CONRAN, *SUPERWOMAN*

I have a rare intolerance to herbs which means I can
only drink fermented liquids, such as gin.

**JULIE WALTERS**

⠿

There was a greasy toad in an equally greasy hole,
and a bacon and egg pie so dry and powdery that it was
like eating a crumbling seventeenth-century wattle
and daub cottage.

**DAVID NOBBS ON THE WARTIME FOOD AT HIS PREP SCHOOL**

⠿

The two biggest sellers in any bookstore are the
cookbooks and the diet books. The cookbooks tell you
how to prepare the food, and the diet books tell you
how not to eat any of it.

**ANDY ROONEY**

⠿

Edmund Blackadder: What on earth was I drinking last
night? My head feels like there's a Frenchman living in it.

**RICHARD CURTIS AND BEN ELTON, WRITERS, *BLACKADDER***

⠿

My mother tells me she's worn out pouring tinned
sauce over the frozen chicken.

**MAEVE BINCHY**

⠿

I formed a new group called Alcoholics Unanimous.
If you don't feel like a drink, you ring another member
and he comes over to persuade you.

RICHARD HARRIS

I will not eat oysters. I want my food dead – not sick,
not wounded – dead.

WOODY ALLEN

For a long time I thought coq au vin meant love in a lorry.

VICTORIA WOOD

I owe it all to little chocolate doughnuts.

JOHN BELUSHI

You notice how they always put the fruit and veg at the
entrance to the supermarket? You go in thinking 'this is a
fresh shop, everything in here is FRESH. I will do well to
shop here.' You never go straight to the bit with the toilet
paper, loo brushes and such, do you? You'd think 'this is a
POO shop! Everything in here is themed on POO!'

EDDIE IZZARD

# THE GOD THING

How can I believe in God when just last week I got my tongue caught in the roller of an electric typewriter?

**WOODY ALLEN**

❖

Ever noticed how people who believe in creationism look really unevolved?

**BILL HICKS**

❖

If we're all God's children, what's so special about Jesus?

**JIMMY CARR**

❖

I've a definite sense of spirituality. I want Brooklyn to be christened, but don't know into what religion yet.

**DAVID BECKHAM**

❖

I don't believe in angels and I have trouble with the whole God thing. I don't want to say I don't believe in God, but I don't think I do. But I believe in people who do.

**BILLY CONNOLLY**

❖

In the beginning there was nothing. God said, 'Let there be light!' And there was light. There was still nothing, but you could see it a whole lot better.

**ELLEN DEGENERES**

When we talk to God, we're praying. When God talks to us, we're schizophrenic.

**LILY TOMLIN**

In real life, Diane Keaton believes in God. But she also believes that the radio works because there are tiny people inside it.

**WOODY ALLEN**

See, the problem is that God gives men a brain and a penis, and only enough blood to run one at a time.

**ROBIN WILLIAMS**

My idea of a good Christian is a priest who can speed-read the Mass, not a semi-demented American with a permanent grin.

**HARRY ENFIELD**

When I found out I thought God was white,
and a man, I lost interest.

**ALICE WALKER**

::

All religions are the same: basically guilt,
with different holidays.

**CATHY LADMAN**

::

Do you think God gets stoned? I think so . . .
look at the platypus.

**ROBIN WILLIAMS**

::

Between projects I go into the park and bite the grass and
wail, 'Why do You make me aware of the fact that I have
to die one day?' God says, 'Please, I have Chinese people
yelling at me, I haven't time for this.' I say all right.
God is like a Jewish waiter, he has too many tables.

**MEL BROOKS, QUOTED IN *THE GUARDIAN*, 1984**

::

I'm not Jewish – it's just that a tree fell on me.

**SPIKE MILLIGAN**

::

Moses was brave, coming down from that mountain
and saying to the Israelites, 'I've got him down to ten!'

**TOM O'CONNOR**

Ⓜ

If there is no God, who pops up the next Kleenex?

**ART HOPPE**

Ⓜ

And God said, 'Let there be light,' and there was light,
but the Electricity Board said He would have to wait until
Thursday to be connected.

**SPIKE MILLIGAN**

Ⓜ

The Catholic Church is still very angry about
*The Da Vinci Code* – they don't like anything that
makes more money in a weekend than they do.

**JAY LENO**

Ⓜ

The one story from Sunday School that sticks in my
head is the story of the baby Jesus having no crib for a bed.
How sad is that? Correct me if I'm wrong but this
Joseph guy – he was a carpenter, wasn't he?

**BRUCE CLARK**

Ⓜ

A lot of Christians wear crosses around their necks.
You think when Jesus comes back he ever wants
to see a fucking cross? It's like going up to Jackie Onassis
wearing a rifle pendant.

BILL HICKS

■■

When you come to Heritage USA, remember to bring
your Bible and your Visa card – because the Bible is the
Holy Truth, and God doesn't take American Express.

JIM BAKKER, AMERICAN TELEVISION EVANGELIST AND FOUNDER
OF HERITAGE USA, A CHRISTIAN THEME PARK

■■

If only God would give me some clear sign! Like
making a large deposit in my name at a Swiss bank.

WOODY ALLEN, *WITHOUT FEATHERS*

■■

I'm an atheist . . . thank God.

DAVE ALLEN

■■

When I was a kid I used to pray every night for a new bicycle. Then I realized that the Lord doesn't work that way, so I stole one and asked Him to forgive me.

**EMO PHILIPS**

::

They say God has existed from the beginning and will exist beyond the end of time. Can you imagine trying to sit through his home movies?

**SCOTT ROEBEN**

::

Born again?! No, I'm not. Excuse me for getting it right the first time.

**DENNIS MILLER**

::

What do atheists scream when they come?

**BILL HICKS**

::

When I told the people of Northern Ireland that I was an atheist, a woman in the audience stood up and said, 'Yes, but is it the God of the Catholics or the God of the Protestants in whom you don't believe?'

**QUENTIN CRISP**

::

I admire the Pope. I have a lot of respect for anyone who can tour without an album.

RITA RUDNER

If it turns out that there is a God, I don't think that he's evil. But the worst that you can say about him is that basically he's an underachiever.

WOODY ALLEN, *LOVE AND DEATH*

# INFLATED EGOS

I'm not going to have some reporters pawing through
our papers. We are the president.

**HILLARY CLINTON**

▪▪

We have become a grandmother.

**MARGARET THATCHER**

▪▪

In 1969 I published a small book on Humility.
It was a pioneering work which has not, to my
knowledge, been superseded.

**LORD LONGFORD**

▪▪

It matters not whether you win or lose; what
matters is whether *I* win or lose.

**DARRIN WEINBERG**

▪▪

So I was smacked out on the Prime Minister's jet, big deal.

**WILL SELF, AFTER TAKING HEROIN ON BOARD JOHN MAJOR'S
PLANE DURING THE 1997 ELECTION CAMPAIGN**

▪▪

What is the play about? It's about to make
me a great deal of money.

TOM STOPPARD

::

There are people who don't like capitalism, and people
who don't like PCs. But there's no one who likes the
PC who doesn't like Microsoft.

BILL GATES

::

Of course they have, or I wouldn't be sitting here
talking to someone like you.

BARBARA CARTLAND, WHEN ASKED BY AN INTERVIEWER IF SHE
THOUGHT BRITISH CLASS BARRIERS HAD COME DOWN

::

Don't worry. I'm not being condescending. I'm far
too busy thinking about important things you
wouldn't understand.

JIMMY CARR

::

Everything I do, I feel is genius.
Whether it is or it isn't.

RUFUS WAINWRIGHT

::

We have top players and, sorry if I'm arrogant,
we have a top manager.

**JOSÉ MOURINHO**

■■

I think that the film *Clueless* was very deep.
I think it was deep in the way that it was very light.
I think lightness has to come from a very deep
place if it's true lightness.

**ALICIA SILVERSTONE**

■■

I could go on stage and make a pizza and
still they'd come to see me.

**FRANK SINATRA**

■■

I am extraordinarily patient, provided I get
my own way in the end.

**MARGARET THATCHER**

■■

I have little patience with anyone who is not self-satisfied.
I am always pleased to see my friends, happy to be with my
wife and family, but the high spot of every day is when
I first catch a glimpse of myself in the shaving mirror.

**ROBERT MORLEY, *PLAYBOY*, 1979**

■■

When I read something saying I've not done anything as good as *Catch-22*, I'm tempted to reply, 'Who has?'

**JOSEPH HELLER**

When did I realize I was God? Well, I was praying and I suddenly realized I was talking to myself.

**PETER O'TOOLE**

It is better to be a has-been than a never-was.

**CECIL PARKINSON**

I have always been a huge admirer of my own work.
I'm one of the funniest and most entertaining writers I know.

**MEL BROOKS**

The spotlight will always be on me, but it's something I'm learning to live with as the years go by.

**DAVID BECKHAM**

I know who you are, and I am not impressed.

**JOAN JETT**

All of the women on *The Apprentice* flirted with me –
consciously or unconsciously. That's to be expected.

**DONALD TRUMP**

❈

Let's face it: God has a big ego problem. Why do
we always have to worship him?

**BILL MAHER**

❈

I just broke up with someone and the last thing she
said to me was, 'You'll never find anyone like me again!'
I'm thinking, 'I should hope not! If I don't want you,
why would I want someone like you?'

**LARRY MILLER**

❈

As God once said, and I think rightly . . .

**MARGARET THATCHER**

❈

# POLITICS

The Pentagon, that immense monument to modern
man's subservience to the desk.

**OLIVER FRANKS**

::

Being an MP feeds your vanity and starves your self-respect.

**MATTHEW PARRIS**

::

Democracy means that anyone can grow up to be president
and anyone who doesn't grow up can be vice-president.

**JOHNNY CARSON**

::

I did not vote Labour because they've heard of Oasis
and nobody is going to vote Tory because William Hague
has got a baseball cap.

**BEN ELTON**

::

If the word 'No' was removed from the English language,
Ian Paisley would be speechless.

**JOHN HUME**

::

Politics: 'Poli' a Latin word meaning 'many', and 'tics' meaning 'bloodsucking creatures.'

ROBIN WILLIAMS

■■

Any American who is prepared to run for president should automatically, by definition, be disqualified from ever doing so.

GORE VIDAL

■■

'Rabbi, can one build socialism in one country?' 'Yes, my son, but one must live in another.'

ANONYMOUS

■■

If I saw Mr Haughey buried at midnight at a crossroads, with a stake driven through his heart – politically speaking – I should continue to wear a clove of garlic round my neck, just in case.

CONOR CRUISE O'BRIEN

■■

The cardinal rule of politics – never get caught in bed with a live man or a dead woman.

LARRY HAGMAN

■■

I believe Ronald Reagan can make this country what it once was . . . a large Arctic region covered with ice.

STEVE MARTIN

■■

The only safe pleasure for a parliamentarian is a bag of boiled sweets.

JULIAN CRITCHLEY

■■

Politics is show business for ugly people.

BRIAN BELO, WINNER OF BIG BROTHER 8

■■

My fellow Americans, I am pleased to tell you I have just signed legislation that will outlaw Russia forever. We begin bombing in five minutes.

RONALD REAGAN, DURING A REHEARSAL FOR A TV BROADCAST THAT WAS SHOWN IN ERROR, 1984

■■

And now the really difficult part: we have to rebuild Iraq into a strong and independent nation that will one day hate the United States.

DAVID LETTERMAN

■■

Diplomacy is the art of letting somebody else have your way.

**DAVID FROST**

##

The trouble with the Conservative Party is they are actually
going backwards. They have now skipped a generation.
At this rate the next leader will have to be exhumed.

**RORY BREMNER**

##

The only decent diplomat is a deaf Trappist.

**JOHN LE CARRÉ**

##

TB [Tony Blair] left it, so then the answering machine
kicked in and GB's [Gordon Brown's] disembodied voice
came on: 'Tony. It's Gordon. I'm locked in the toilet.'

**ALASTAIR CAMPBELL, *THE BLAIR YEARS***

##

You'll notice that Nancy Reagan never drinks
water when Ronnie speaks.

**ROBIN WILLIAMS**

##

Richard Nixon means never having to say you're sorry.

**WILFRED SHEED**

##

The whole point of elected heads of state is supposed to be that they are chosen by a majority. And that they are not the idiot children of previous heads of state. When the most powerful man in the world makes David Beckham look like Chomsky, one might hanker after one of those progressive Nordic monarchs who cycle to work and give cannabis to the poor. One suspects that Bush only stood for election because he misread the word as 'electrocution' and knew that's something he likes.

JEREMY HARDY

The only possible way there'd be an uprising in this country would be if they banned car boot sales and caravanning.

VICTORIA WOOD

I'm a fan of President Nixon. I worship the quicksand he walks on.

ART BUCHWALD

When I go into the voting booth, do I vote for the person who is the best president? Or the slime bucket who will make my life as a cartoonist wonderful?

MIKE PETERS

A typical speech by Margaret Thatcher sounds like the Book of Revelations read over a railway station public address system by a headmistress of a certain age wearing calico knickers.

CLIVE JAMES

The Christmas tree was delivered to the White House yesterday. Just what we need at the White House, more dead wood.

DAVID LETTERMAN

I should prefer to have a politician who regularly went to a massage parlour than one who promised a laptop computer for every teacher.

A. N. WILSON

Earlier today, President Bush met with the head of one of Iraq's Shiite political parties. However, there was an awkward moment when Bush asked him, 'Are you the Shiite head?'

CONAN O'BRIEN

The function of socialism is to raise suffering to a higher level.

NORMAN MAILER

Saying we're in a slow recovery, not a recession, is like saying we don't have any unemployed – we just have a lot of people who are really, really late for work.

**JAY LENO**

▪▪

War is the only issue that excites our base.

**KARL ROVE**

▪▪

As far as I am concerned, dirty tricks are part and parcel of effective government.

**ALAN CLARK**

▪▪

There's a huge trust. I see it all the time when people come up to me and say, 'I don't want you to let me down again.'

**GEORGE W. BUSH**

▪▪

Bill Clinton is going to tie the whole thing [the Northern Ireland Peace Process] up. He's going to come over and sort it out because he's got a lot in common with the people of Northern Ireland, as 69 was the start of our troubles as well.

**PATRICK KIELTY**

▪▪

# ANIMAL MAGIC

Cats have nine lives. Which makes them
ideal for experimentation.

**JIMMY CARR**

■■

To my mind, the only possible pet is a cow. Cows love
you . . . They will listen to your problems and never ask a
thing in return. They will be your friends forever. And when
you get tired of them, you can kill and eat them. Perfect.

**BILL BRYSON, *NEITHER HERE NOR THERE***

■■

Grouse shooting begins on August 12th. A grouse
shot before that date tends to be very annoyed.

**MICHAEL SHEA**

■■

Before birds get sucked into jet engines, do they ever
think, 'Is that Rod Stewart in first class?'

**EDDIE IZZARD**

■■

A dolphin will jump out of the water for a piece
of fish; imagine what he'd do for some chips.

**HARRY HILL**

■■

A dog is not intelligent. Never trust an animal
that's surprised by its own farts.

**FRANK SKINNER**

■■

Dogs have no money. Isn't that amazing? They're broke
their entire lives. But they get through. You know
why dogs have no money? No pockets.

**JERRY SEINFELD**

■■

The lion and the calf shall lie down together, but
the calf won't get much sleep.

**WOODY ALLEN**

■■

If we aren't supposed to eat animals then why are
they made out of meat?

**JO BRAND**

■■

The stick insect has sex for 79 days straight. If it's only
been 77 days, is that a quickie? And you know that even
after 79 days, the female goes, 'Oh, so close!' And the
guy tells his buddies it was 158 days.

**JAY LENO**

■■

Who was the first person to look at a cow and say,
'I think I'll squeeze these dangly things here and
drink whatever comes out?'

PETER KAY

■■

Every day, the dog and I, we go for a tramp in the woods.
And he loves it! Mind you, the tramp is getting a bit fed up!

JERRY DENNIS

■■

What is it with chimpanzees and that middle parting?
Stuck in the twenties, aren't they?

HARRY HILL

■■

Horseshoes are lucky. Horses have four bits of lucky
nailed to their feet. They should be the luckiest animals in
the world. They should rule the country. They should win
all the races at least. 'In the fifth race today, every single
horse was first equal . . . one horse threw a shoe, came
third . . . the duck was ninth . . . and five ran.'

EDDIE IZZARD

■■

The right to bear arms is slightly less ludicrous than
the right to arm bears.

CHRIS ADDISON

■■

I have a dog that's half pitbull, half poodle.
Not much of a guard dog, but a vicious gossip.

**CRAIG SHOEMAKER**

Two guys were watching a dog lick himself, and one said,
'I wish I could do that.' The other replied,
'Maybe you should pet him first.'

**DOUG BENSON**

Every woman should have four pets in her life.
A mink in her closet, a jaguar in her garage, a tiger in her
bed, and a jackass who pays for everything.

**PARIS HILTON**

The sooner all the animals are extinct, the sooner
we'll find their money.

**ED BLUESTONE**

Dogs feel very strongly that they should always go with
you in the car, in case the need should arise for them
to bark violently at nothing right in your ear.

**DAVE BARRY**

I am an evil giraffe, and I shall eat more leaves from this tree than perhaps I should, so that other giraffes may die.

EDDIE IZZARD

▮▮

Did you ever walk into a room and forget why you walked in? I think that's how dogs spend their lives.

SUE MURPHY

▮▮

If toast always lands butter-side down, and cats always land on their feet, what happens if you strap toast on the back of a cat and drop it?

STEVEN WRIGHT

▮▮

I was such an ugly kid – when I played in the sandbox, the cat kept covering me up.

RODNEY DANGERFIELD

▮▮

All bears are agile, cunning and immensely strong, and they are always hungry. If they want to kill you and eat you, they can, and pretty much whenever they want. This doesn't happen often, but – and here is the absolutely salient point – once would be enough.

BILL BRYSON, *A WALK IN THE WOODS*

▮▮

It's not pining, it's passed on. This parrot is no more.
It has ceased to be. It's expired and gone to meet its maker.
This is a late parrot. It's a stiff. Bereft of life, it rests in peace.
If you hadn't nailed it to the perch, it would be pushing
up the daisies. It's run down the curtain and joined the choir
invisible. This is an ex-parrot.

**MR PRALINE (JOHN CLEESE),** *MONTY PYTHON'S FLYING CIRCUS*

# HOW VERY INSULTING

David Frost is the bubonic plagiarist.

JONATHAN MILLER

■■

Abi Titmuss? She's been tied to more bedposts than
David Blunkett's dog.

JONATHAN ROSS

■■

Back in London I'd heard Condé Nast referred
to as 'condescending and nasty', but my initial impression
was that beneath its glamorous façade it was just like
any other magazine publishing company. It wasn't long
before I realized my mistake.

TOBY YOUNG, *HOW TO LOSE FRIENDS AND ALIENATE PEOPLE*

■■

Michael Moore simultaneously represents everything
I detest in a human being and everything I feel obligated
to defend in an American. Quite simply, it is that stupid
moron's right to be that utterly, completely wrong.

DENNIS MILLER

■■

Boy George is all England needs – another queen
who can't dress.

**JOAN RIVERS**

▪▪

Chevy Chase couldn't ad-lib a fart after a baked-bean dinner.

**JOHNNY CARSON**

▪▪

The last time I was in Spain I got through six Jeffrey Archer
novels. I must remember to take enough toilet paper
next time.

**BOB MONKHOUSE**

▪▪

I have a television set in every room of the house
but one. There has to be some place you can go when
Bob Monkhouse is on.

**BENNY HILL**

▪▪

The only genius with an IQ of 60.

**GORE VIDAL ON ANDY WARHOL**

▪▪

She was a really bad-looking girl. Facially,
she resembled Louis Armstrong's voice.

**WOODY ALLEN**

▪▪

Many people would no more think of entering
journalism than the sewage business – which at
least does us all some good.

STEPHEN FRY

⠿

After making love I said to my girl, 'Was it good for you too?'
And she said, 'I don't think this was good for anybody.'

GARRY SHANDLING

⠿

A self-important, boring, flash-in-the-pan Brit.

ROBERT DOWNEY JNR ON HUGH GRANT

⠿

George W. Bush says he spends sixty to ninety minutes
a day working out. He says he works out because it clears
his mind. Sometimes just a little too much.

JAY LENO

⠿

Jeffrey Archer is proof of the proposition that
in each of us there lurks a bad novel.

JULIAN CRITCHLEY

⠿

To call him grey would be an insult to porridge.

SIR NICHOLAS FAIRBAIRN ON JOHN MAJOR

⠿

Once in every lifetime a really beautiful song comes along . . .
Until it does, I'd like to do this one.

**CLIFF RICHARD**

Keanu Reeves is going to play Superman in a new movie.
The villains don't use kryptonite to stop him,
they just use big words.

**CONAN O'BRIEN**

There was nothing wrong with you that a vasectomy
of the vocal cords wouldn't fix.

**LISA ALTHER**

Phyllis Diller's so ancient she's just a carcass with a mouth.

**RUBY WAX**

Rock journalism is people who can't write interviewing
people who can't talk for people who can't read.

**FRANK ZAPPA**

He has left his body to science –
and science is contesting the will.

**DAVID FROST**

I'm going to send him an ice bucket, with a note attached –
'Stick your head in it' – instead of the champagne.

**PHILIP GREEN ON STUART ROSE, CHIEF EXECUTIVE OF
MARKS & SPENCER**

※

To listen even briefly to Ronald Reagan is to realize
that he is a man upon whose synapses the termites
have dined long and well.

**CHRISTOPHER HITCHENS**

※

Prince looks like a dwarf who's been dipped
in a bucket of pubic hair.

**BOY GEORGE**

※

Paul Getty ... had always been vastly, immeasurably
wealthy, and yet went about looking like a man who
cannot quite remember whether he remembered
to turn the gas off before leaving home.

**BERNARD LEVIN**

※

Every year, President Bush gets to pardon one turkey,
and this year it was Donald Rumsfeld.

**DAVID LETTERMAN**

※

Princess Anne is such an active lass. So outdoorsy.
She loves nature in spite of what nature did to her.

**BETTE MIDLER**

Let's face it, Elizabeth Taylor's last marriage was all
about selling perfume because it's hard to sell perfume
when you're a fat old spinster.

**JOHNNY ROTTEN**

Television is to news what bumper stickers are to philosophy.

**RICHARD NIXON**

It is said that swimming develops poise and grace,
but have you seen how a duck walks?

**WOODY ALLEN**

Countryside: the killing of Piers Morgan.

**STEPHEN FRY**

My fifty years have shown me that few people know
what they are talking about. I don't mean idiots
who don't know. I mean everyone.

**JOHN CLEESE**

Every word she writes is a lie,
including 'and' and 'the'.

MARY MCCARTHY ON LILLIAN HELLMAN

∷

Orgasm for peace? Wasn't that Clinton's foreign policy?

JAY LENO

∷

*Racial Characteristics:* hard to tell a Canadian
from an extremely boring regular white person unless
he's dressed to go outdoors. Very little is known of the
Canadian country since it is rarely visited by anyone
but the Queen and illiterate sport fishermen.

P. J. O'ROURKE, 'FOREIGNERS AROUND THE WORLD',
*NATIONAL LAMPOON*, 1976

∷

A triumph of the embalmer's art.

GORE VIDAL ON RONALD REAGAN

∷

When you look at Prince Charles, don't you
think that someone in the Royal family knew
someone in the Royal family?

ROBIN WILLIAMS

∷

# SEXUAL POLITICS

Clinton lied. A man might forget where he parks
or where he lives, but he never forgets oral sex,
no matter how bad it is.

BARBARA BUSH

▪▪

By staying single I have one saintly virtue as far
as men are concerned, even though it is by default:
I can't be unfaithful to one of their sex.

IRMA KURTZ

▪▪

If a woman tells you she's twenty and she looks sixteen,
she's twelve. If she tells you she's twenty-six
and looks twenty-six, she's damn near forty.

CHRIS ROCK

▪▪

The company's policy on sexual harassment isn't a
concession to the feminist sensibilities of its female
employees; it's designed to protect them from men who
earn less than $500,000 a year.

TOBY YOUNG, *HOW TO LOSE FRIENDS AND ALIENATE PEOPLE*

▪▪

CNN found that Hillary Clinton is the most admired woman in America. Women admire her because she's strong and successful. Men admire her because she allows her husband to cheat and get away with it.

JAY LENO

■■

There's very little advice in men's magazines, because men don't think there's a lot they don't know. Women do. Women want to learn. Men think, 'I know what I'm doing, just show me somebody naked.'

JERRY SEINFELD

■■

We have lived through the era when happiness was a warm puppy, and the era when happiness was a dry martini, and now we have come to the era when happiness is 'knowing what your uterus looks like'.

NORA EPHRON, *CRAZY SALAD*

■■

It took women's liberation to make me realize that women can be just as rotten and lousy as men.

NORMAN MAILER

■■

I've never won an argument with her; and the only times I thought I had I found out the argument wasn't over yet.

JIMMY CARTER

■■

Women should have labels on their foreheads saying
'Government Health Warning: women can seriously damage
your brains, genitals, current account, confidence, razor
blades, and good standing among your friends.'

JEFFREY BERNARD

■■

'I hate discussions of feminism that end up with
who does the dishes,' she said. So do I. But at the end,
there are always the damned dishes.

MARILYN FRENCH, *THE WOMEN'S ROOM*

■■

If women ran the world we wouldn't have wars,
just intense negotiations every twenty-eight days.

ROBIN WILLIAMS

■■

Monica Geller: This is not even a date. It's just two
people going out to dinner and not having sex.
Chandler Bing: Sounds like a date to me.

JEFFREY ASTROF AND MIKE SIKOWITZ, WRITERS, *FRIENDS*

■■

Don't have sex, man. It leads to kissing and pretty
soon you have to start talking to them.

STEVE MARTIN

■■

In my youth there were words you couldn't say
in front of a girl; now you can't say 'girl'.

**TOM LEHRER**

Years ago, manhood was an opportunity for achievement,
and now it is a problem to be overcome.

**GARRISON KEILLOR, *THE BOOK OF GUYS***

A smart girl is one who knows how to play tennis,
piano and dumb.

**LYNN REDGRAVE**

I didn't fight to get women out from behind the vacuum
cleaner to get them on to the board of Hoover.

**GERMAINE GREER**

My biological clock is ticking so loud I'm nearly deafened
by it. They search me going into planes.

**MARIAN KEYES, *LAST CHANCE SALOON***

You don't know a woman till you've met her in court.

**NORMAN MAILER**

Here's how men think. Sex, work – and those are reversible,
depending on age – sex, work, food, sports and lastly,
begrudgingly, relationships. And here's how women think.
Relationships, relationships, relationships, work, sex,
shopping, weight, food.

CARRIE FISHER, *SURRENDER THE PINK*

I suppose true sexual equality will come when a
general called Anthea is found having an unwise lunch
with a young, unreliable male model from Spain.

JOHN MORTIMER

How much fame, money and power does a woman
have to achieve on her own before you can punch
her in the face?

P. J. O'ROURKE, *MODERN MANNERS*

Only in America do these peasants, our mothers, get their
hair dyed platinum at the age of sixty, and walk up and
down Collins Avenue in Florida in pedal pushers and mink
stoles – and with opinions on every subject under the sun. It
isn't their fault they were given a gift like speech – look, if
cows could talk, they would say things just as idiotic.

PHILIP ROTH

Even the most powerful lie detector invented couldn't drag a secret out of a woman, however, women rarely have lunch with lie detectors.

DANNY MCCROSSAN

**::**

Anyone can have the key to the executive washroom, but once a woman gets inside, what is there? A lavatory.

GERMAINE GREER

**::**

Women now have choices. The can be married, not married, have a job, not have a job, be married with children, unmarried with children. Men have the same choice we've always had: work or prison.

TIM ALLEN

**::**

The feminist movement seems to have beaten the manners out of men, but I didn't see them put up a lot of resistance.

CLARISSA DICKSON WRIGHT

**::**

Hillary Clinton and Nancy Reagan have a lot in common – they're both smarter than their husbands and both consulted the stars for guidance: Nancy with astrology and Hillary with Barbra Streisand.

BILL MAHER

**::**

See women need to talk because they feel like they have to have adequate levels of communication in order to sustain a healthy and open relationship, whereas men are only driven to speak because of matters beyond their control, like not being able to find clean socks.

DANNY McCROSSAN

# HOW SCANDALOUS

Scandal is something that brings society together.
**MAX CLIFFORD**

::

I have expressed a degree of regret that
could be equated with an apology.
**DES BROWNE, BRITISH DEFENCE SECRETARY, AFTER
ROYAL NAVY SAILORS SOLD THEIR STORIES HAVING BEEN
HELD HOSTAGE IN IRAN, 2007**

::

I think we have explored the further reaches of 'for
better or worse' far more than some other couples.
**MARY ARCHER, WHOSE HUSBAND LORD ARCHER
WAS TRIED FOR PERJURY IN 2001**

::

I wasn't hungry, but I was angry, lonely and tired.
**BILL CLINTON ON MONICA LEWINSKY**

::

Watergate is an immensely complicated scandal with a cast of
characters as varied as a Tolstoy novel.
**BOB WOODWARD, CO-AUTHOR OF *ALL THE PRESIDENT'S MEN***

::

Researchers have found that oral sex among teenagers
has doubled in the last ten years. So who says there
is no lasting Clinton legacy?

**JAY LENO**

Exclusives aren't what they used to be. We tend to put
'exclusive' on everything just to annoy other papers.
I once put exclusive on the weather by mistake.

**PIERS MORGAN**

My friends, as I have discovered myself, there are
no disasters, only opportunities. And, indeed,
opportunities for fresh disasters.

**BORIS JOHNSON, FORMER SHADOW ARTS MINISTER,
AFTER HIS AFFAIR WITH PETRONELLA WYATT**

Some mornings, it's just not worth chewing
through the leather straps.

**EMO PHILIPS**

When one door closes, another one falls on
top of you.

**ANGUS DEAYTON**

We are not without accomplishment.
We have managed to distribute poverty equally.

NGUYEN CO THATCH, VIETNAMESE FOREIGN MINISTER

When I want a peerage, I shall buy one
like an honest man.

LORD NORTHCLIFFE

I am part man, part cyborg. You'd be surprised
at the parts I've had inserted in me. Perhaps that's
why I walk a little stiffly.

GRAHAM NORTON

There are double standards even today. A man can sleep
around and nobody asks any questions; a woman, you make
nineteen, twenty mistakes and right away you're a tramp!

JOAN RIVERS

She was a highly sexed woman who had ceased to
be satisfied with normal relations and had started
to indulge in disgusting sexual activities to gratify a
debased sexual appetite.

LORD WHEATLEY'S COMMENT WHILE SUMMING UP THE
DIVORCE OF THE DUKE AND DUCHESS OF ARGYLL IN 1963

# GOOD ADVICE

If you think squash is a competitive activity,
try flower arrangement.

**ALAN BENNETT, *TALKING HEADS***

::

Never transmit a sexual disease in public.

**P. J. O'ROURKE, *MODERN MANNERS***

::

Never go to a dentist with blood in his hair.
Never holiday in a country where they still point at planes.

**WILLIAM RUSHTON**

::

Even if you have only two seconds, drop everything
and give him a blow job. That way he won't really
want sex with anyone else.

**JERRY HALL**

::

Interviewer: What is your all-time best travel tip?
Ross Noble: If you end up in a Turkish prison, don't
sign up for the ballroom dancing classes.

**ROSS NOBLE, RADIO FOUR INTERVIEW**

::

Running a company on market research is like
driving while looking in the rear-view mirror.

ANITA RODDICK

::

Nothing is illegal if one hundred well-placed
businessmen decide to do it.

ANDREW YOUNG

::

If you're being chased by a police dog, try not to go
through a tunnel, then on to a little seesaw, then jump
through a hoop of fire. They're trained for that.

MILTON JONES

::

No problem is insoluble, given
a big enough plastic bag.

TOM STOPPARD

::

Free your mind, and your bottom will follow.

SARAH, THE DUCHESS OF YORK ON SLIMMING

::

Never, ever go to bed with a man on the first date.
Not ever. Unless you really want to.

CYNTHIA HEIMEL

::

During dinner, it may be necessary to excuse yourself
for a telephone call. However, it is far preferable to
have a phone brought to the table . . . as a general rule,
white telephones go with fish and poultry, and black ones
with anything else. If you are calling during dessert,
a small after-dinner phone should be used . . . if you are
satisfied, say something like, 'Yes, it is a very nice,
light telephone, with a good, clear tone and a smooth,
almost velvety action.'

MISS PIGGY, *MISS PIGGY'S GUIDE TO LIFE*

::

Never keep up with the Joneses. Drag them
down to your level.

QUENTIN CRISP

::

A tip to all new mothers. Don't put your baby in
bed with you because you might fall asleep, roll on it
and put your back out.

HARRY HILL

::

Love hurts. Try a lubricated finger.

JIMMY CARR

::

Never pick a fight with an ugly person;
they've got nothing to lose.

ROBIN WILLIAMS

■■

Bath twice a day to be really clean, once a day to be passably
clean, once a week to avoid being a public menace.

ANTHONY BURGESS

■■

Never wear anything that panics the cat.

P. J. O'ROURKE

■■

Sexual fidelity is not necessary in a well-conducted
marriage. Your eldest son should certainly be your own,
but beyond this it is excessively vulgar to enquire too closely
into the paternity of your children.

SIMON RAVEN

■■

If you stay in a house and you go to the bathroom
and there is no toilet paper, you can always slide down the
banisters. Don't tell me you haven't done it.

PAUL MERTON

■■

Never get into a narrow double bed with a wide single man.

QUENTIN CRISP

■■

Never trust a man who, when he's alone in a room
with a tea cosy, doesn't try it on.

BILLY CONNOLLY

■■

From my experience of life I believe my personal
motto should be 'Beware of men bearing flowers.'

MURIEL SPARK, *CURRICULUM VITAE*

■■

When a couple decide to divorce, they should
inform both sets of parents before having a party
and telling all their friends. This is not only courteous
but practical. Parents may be very willing to pitch
in with comments, criticism and malicious gossip
of their own to help the divorce.

P. J. O'ROURKE

■■

# VROOM, VROOM!

When I'm driving and I see a sign that says, 'CAUTION: SMALL CHILDREN PLAYING' I slow down.
And then it occurs to me, I'm not afraid of small children.

**JONATHAN KATZ**

■■

To my wife, double parking means on top of another car.

**DAVE BARRY**

■■

I know a lot about cars, man. I can look at any car's headlights and tell you exactly which way it's coming.

**MITCH HEDBERG**

■■

Unfortunately I can't drive. Or rather I can, but nobody believes in my ability enough to give me a licence.

**CLIVE JAMES, *FLYING VISITS***

■■

There are a number of mechanical devices which increase sexual arousal, particularly in women. Chief among these is the Mercedes-Benz 380SL convertible.

**P. J. O'ROURKE**

■■

The interior of the [Aston Martin] V8 may be surprisingly cramped but, despite that, this is not a car for small people. You'd look stupid driving this unless you were at least 6 foot 3 inches and 14 stone. Other people who would look stupid in it include Liberal Democrats, Freemasons, folk singers, nancy-boy footballers, vicars, scoutmasters, people who like DIY or Michael Bolton, women, environmentalists and anyone who has ever been to a poetry reading. You can't even think about driving this car if you like salad. Socialists are right out. So are people who use the words 'toilet', 'nourishing' or 'settee' . . . The V8 is for those of us who like our beer brown and our fags to be high on tar and low on lentils.

JEREMY CLARKSON, *BORN TO BE RILED*

■■

Am I the only person who gets confused about the amount of alcohol you can safely drink before driving and the amount of alcohol you can take through customs?

HARRY HILL

■■

I would think the less time you have left in life, the faster you should drive. I think old people should be allowed to drive their age. If you're 80, do 80. If you're 100, do 100.

JERRY SEINFELD

■■

. . . there are two types of car owners. The first type is
those who left school early. Such people crawl under stopped
cars, adjust the grommets, strip down the carburettor
manifold, suck petrol through the sump gasket, spit it out
manfully and make the car go. The other type is the educated
few. We are strong on the ontological insecurity of
nineteenth-century novelists. When our cars stop, we ring
the AA as soon as we have finished crying.

JOE BENNETT, *FUN RUN AND OTHER OXYMORONS*

▪▪

Sex is more fun than cars, but cars
refuel quicker than men.

GERMAINE GREER

▪▪

I sit in the traffic trying to get out of the centre of
Killarney. It's a slow business. If aliens landed, you'd
be hard pressed to explain to them the difference
between Killarney traffic, and parking.

PETE McCARTHY, *McCARTHY'S BAR*

▪▪

I couldn't repair your brakes, so I made your horn louder.

STEVEN WRIGHT

▪▪

When a man opens the car door for his wife,
it's either a new car or a new wife.

PRINCE PHILIP, DUKE OF EDINBURGH

▪▪

Men drive too fast, we were told, because the car is an
extension of the penis. But if it were, men would surely
not drive too fast; they would just back in and out of the
garage. Or maybe just polish it all the time.

JEREMY HARDY

▪▪

Are there keys to a plane? Maybe that's what those
delays are sometimes, when you're just sitting there at the
gate. Maybe the pilot sits up there in the cockpit going,
'Oh, I don't believe this. Dammit, I did it again.'
They tell you it's something mechanical because they
don't want to come on the P.A. system: 'Ladies and
gentlemen, we're going to be delayed here on the ground
for a while. I, uh . . . Oh, God this is so embarrassing . . . I,
I left the keys to the plane in my apartment.
They're in this big ashtray by the front door.
I'm sorry, I'll run back and get them.'

JERRY SEINFELD

▪▪

I know some people are against drunk driving,
but you know, sometimes you've just got no choice.
Those kids gotta get to school . . .

**DAVE ATTELL**

▓

Never lend your car to anyone to whom
you have given birth.

**ERMA BOMBECK**

▓

I can't swim. I can't drive, either. I was going to learn to drive
but then I thought, well, what if I crash into a lake?

**DYLAN MORAN**

▓

Racing cars which have been converted for road use
never really work. It's like making a hardcore adult film,
and then editing it so that it can be shown in British hotels.
You'd just end up with a sort of half-hour close-up of some
bloke's sweaty face.

**JEREMY CLARKSON**

▓

# RELATIVE VALUES

I owe a lot to my parents – especially my mother and father.

**GREG NORMAN**

⸬

My Hungarian grandfather was the kind of man that could follow someone into a revolving door and come out first.

**STEPHEN FRY**

⸬

My God, we've had cloning in the South for years.
It's called cousins.

**ROBIN WILLIAMS**

⸬

There must be many fathers around the country who have experienced the cruellest, most crushing rejection of all: their children have ended up supporting the wrong team.

**NICK HORNBY, *FEVER PITCH***

⸬

I have four sons and three stepsons. I have learnt what it is like to step on Lego with bare feet.

**FAY WELDON**

⸬

My mum was a ventriloquist and she was always
throwing her voice. For ten years I thought the dog
was telling me to kill my father.

**PETER KAY**

I'm a godmother, that's a great thing to be, a godmother.
She calls me god for short, that's cute. I taught her that.

**ELLEN DEGENERES**

When Mel Brooks told his mother that he was marrying an
Italian girl, she said, 'Bring her over, I'll be in the kitchen –
with my head in the oven!'

**ANNE BANCROFT**

My brother has an unusual job – he finds things
before other people lose them.

**FRANK CARSON**

My wife said, 'Can my mother come down for the
weekend?' I said, 'Why?' She said, 'Well, she's been
up on the roof two weeks already.'

**BOB MONKHOUSE**

My mother never saw the irony in calling me a son-of-a-bitch.

**JACK NICHOLSON**

If you want to recapture your youth, just cut off his allowance.

**AL BERNSTEIN**

Where there's a will – there's a relative.

**RICKY GERVAIS**

The one thing I remember about Christmas was that my father used to take me out in a boat about ten miles offshore on Christmas Day, and I used to have to swim back. Extraordinary. It was a ritual. Mind you, that wasn't the hard part. The difficult bit was getting out of the sack.

**JOHN CLEESE**

Maybe there is no actual place called hell. Maybe hell is just having to listen to our grandparents breathe through their noses when they're eating sandwiches.

**JIM CARREY**

My father had a profound influence on me. He was a lunatic.

**SPIKE MILLIGAN**

Sure I love Liam – but not as much as I love Pot Noodle.

NOEL GALLAGHER ON HIS BROTHER

■■

Dear Ann,
I have a problem. I have two brothers. One brother is
in television. The other was put to death in the electric
chair for murder. My mother died from insanity when
I was three years old. My sisters are prostitutes and my
father sells drugs to high-school students. Recently, I
met a girl who was just released from a reformatory
where she had served time for smothering her
illegitimate child to death. I want to marry her.

My problem is this. If I marry this girl, should I tell
her about my brother who works in television?

ANONYMOUS

■■

Daphne: Oh, Dr Crane, why is it so easy to love
our family, but so hard to like them?
Frasier: Daphne, that is one of those questions that
makes life so rich and psychiatrists richer.

LINDA MORRIS AND VIC RAUSEO, WRITERS, *FRASIER*

■■

Having one child makes you a parent; having
two you are a referee.

DAVID FROST

■■

My parents warned me never to open the cellar door or
I would see things I shouldn't see. So, one day when they
were out, I did open the cellar door and I did see things
I shouldn't see – grass, flowers, the sun . . .

**EMO PHILIPS**

You see this watch? This is an absolutely fantastic, very
fine, elegant gold watch which speaks of breeding and
was sold to me by my grandfather on his deathbed.

**WOODY ALLEN**

I love being a grandmother. It's great to finally be greeted
by someone who's bald, drooling and wearing a diaper
who's not my date.

**JOAN RIVERS**

My mother hated me. Once she took me to an
orphanage and told me to mingle.

**PHYLLIS DILLER**

Hyacinth Bucket: Richard, you know I love my family, but
that is no reason why I need to acknowledge them in public.

**ROY CLARKE, WRITER, *KEEPING UP APPEARANCES***

I was raised by just my mom. See, my father died
when I was eight years old. At least that's what
he told us in the letter.

**DREW CAREY**

It's funny the way a parent's raised eyebrow can
do more damage to your psyche than, say,
Chinese water torture.

**ARABELLA WEIR, *DOES MY BUM LOOK BIG IN THIS?***

I took my mother-in-law to Madame Tussaud's
Chamber of Horrors and one of the attendants said,
'Keep her moving, sir, we're stocktaking.'

**LES DAWSON**

And let me step back here and say that I was a very
late kid – growing up I had parents who were
much older than I.

**JONATHAN FRANZEN**

My daughter thinks I'm nosy. At least that's
what she says in her diary.

**SALLY POPLIN**

I haven't spoken to my mother-in-law for eighteen months – I don't like to interrupt her.

**KEN DODD**

∷

My family is really boring. They have a coffee-table book called *Pictures We Took Just to Use Up the Rest of the Film*.

**PENELOPE LOMBARD**

∷

If your parents never had children, chances are you won't either.

**DICK CAVETT**

∷

All I heard when I was growing up was, 'Why can't you be more like your cousin Sheila? Why can't you be more like your cousin Sheila?' Sheila died at birth.

**JOAN RIVERS**

∷

When I was kidnapped, my parents snapped into action. They rented out my room.

**WOODY ALLEN**

∷

# FOR BETTER, FOR WORSE

Instead of getting married again, I'm going to
find a woman I don't like and just give her a house.

**ROD STEWART**

■■

Ah, yes, divorce . . . from the Latin word meaning to
rip out a man's genitals through his wallet.

**ROBIN WILLIAMS**

■■

Marriage is like the witness protection programme:
you get all new clothes, you live in the suburbs and
you're not allowed to see your friends anymore.

**JEREMY HARDY**

■■

My boyfriend and I broke up. He wanted to
get married and I didn't want him to.

**RITA RUDNER**

■■

If variety is the spice of life, marriage is
the big can of leftover Spam.

JOHNNY CARSON

⬛

I don't want to give you the idea I'm trying to
hide anything, or that anything unorthodox goes on
between my wife and me. It doesn't. Nothing goes on at
all . . . No foreplay. No afterplay. And fuck all in between.

ALAN BENNETT, *ENJOY*

⬛

I'm not some Tammy Wynette standing by her man.

HILLARY CLINTON

⬛

Personally I know nothing about sex because
I've always been married.

ZSA ZSA GABOR

⬛

Zsa Zsa Gabor got married as a one-off and
it was so successful she turned it into a series.

BOB HOPE

⬛

There are two dilemmas that rattle the human skull:
How do you hang on to someone who won't stay?
And how do you get rid of someone who won't go?

### DANNY DeVITO

▪▪

Men who have a pierced ear are better prepared for marriage
– they've experienced pain and bought jewellery.

### RITA RUDNER

▪▪

I always take my wife morning tea in my pyjamas.
But is she grateful? No, she says she'd rather have it in a cup.

### ERIC MORECAMBE

▪▪

I blame my mother for my poor sex life. All she told
me was 'the man goes on top and the woman underneath.'
For three years my husband and I slept in bunk beds.

### JOAN RIVERS

▪▪

In Pagan times, uninspired people made sacrifices at the
altar, and today, thanks to marriage, many still do.

### DANNY McCROSSAN

▪▪

Ronnie Corbett: Do you think marriage is a lottery?
Ronnie Barker: No. With a lottery you do have
a slight chance.

**THE TWO RONNIES**

■■

Marriage is a wonderful invention; but, then again,
so is a bicycle repair kit.

**BILLY CONNOLLY**

■■

Relationships are a bit like sharks – they have
to keep in motion.

**RICHARD GERE**

■■

Our oldest friends, the Purgavies . . . have been to
stay this week. Over dinner we counted up and realized
that they have been happily married longer than most.
Jane says she has no particular handy hints to pass on,
except she's found it helps to start each new day by
arriving down at breakfast, throwing her arms in the air
and announcing apologetically, 'It's all my fault.'

**ANNE ROBINSON, *THE TIMES*, 1999**

■■

Don't get mad, get everything.

**IVANA TRUMP ON DIVORCE**

■■

I married beneath me. All women do.

**NANCY ASTOR**

∷

If you made a list of reasons why any couple got married, and another list of the reasons for their divorce, you'd have a lot of overlapping.

**MIGNON MCLAUGHLIN**

∷

The difference between divorce and legal separation is that a legal separation gives a husband time to hide his money.

**JOHNNY CARSON**

∷

They think it's your destiny to clean and I guess it's their destiny to have a couch surgically implanted on their behind. You may marry the man of your dreams, ladies, but years later you're married to a couch that burps.

**ROSEANNE BARR**

∷

Michael Douglas likes to have Catherine Zeta-Jones dress up in a French maid's outfit, complete with feather duster. How old is your husband when you have to dust him?

**CRAIG KILBORN**

∷

My mother said it was simple to keep a man: you must
be a maid in the living room, a cook in the kitchen and
a whore in the bedroom. I said I'd hire the other two
and take care of the bedroom bit.

JERRY HALL

Every time I try to make my marriage more exciting,
my wife finds out about it right away.

BOB MONKHOUSE

Marge Simpson: Homer, is this the way you
pictured married life?
Homer Simpson: eah, pretty much. Except that
we drove around in a van solving mysteries.

STEVE TOMPKINS, WRITER, *THE SIMPSONS*

Basically, my wife is immature. I'd be at home in
my bath and she'd come in and sink my boats.

WOODY ALLEN

I thought when I was forty-one I would be married
with kids. Well, to be honest, I thought I'd be divorced
with weekend access.

SEAN HUGHES

# THIS SPORTING LIFE

There are few tactical rules for mixed doubles.
One is to hit the girl whenever possible.

**BILL TILDEN**

■■

The natural state of the football fan is bitter
disappointment, no matter what the score.

**NICK HORNBY, *FEVER PITCH***

■■

Sure there have been injuries and deaths in boxing –
but none of them was serious.

**ALAN MINTER**

■■

Frasier: Have you any idea of appropriate
baseball-watching attire?
Niles: Obviously you failed to detect
the subtle diamond pattern in my tie.

**MICHAEL B. KAPLAN, WRITER, *FRASIER***

■■

In the Bob Hope Golf Classic, the participation of President Gerald Ford was more than enough to remind you that the nuclear button was at one stage at the disposal of a man who might have either pressed it by mistake or else pressed it deliberately in order to obtain room service.

**CLIVE JAMES**

Women playing cricket should treat it as a matter between consenting females in private.

**MICHAEL PARKINSON**

Football hooligans? Well, there are the ninety-two club chairmen, for a start.

**BRIAN CLOUGH**

Jogging is for people who aren't intelligent enough to watch breakfast television.

**VICTORIA WOOD**

If you're a sporting star, you're a sporting star. If you don't quite make it, you become a coach. If you can't coach, you become a journalist. If you can't spell, you introduce *Grandstand* on a Saturday afternoon.

**DES LYNAM**

It's a funny kind of month, October.
For the really keen cricket fan it's when you discover
that your wife left you in May.

**DENIS NORDEN**

■■

I love fishing. It's like transcendental
meditation with a punchline.

**BILLY CONNOLLY**

■■

Monica Seles – I'd hate to be next door to
her on her wedding night.

**SIR PETER USTINOV COMMENTING ON SELES'S PENCHANT
FOR GRUNTING WHILE PLAYING TENNIS**

■■

Winning is everything. The only ones who remember you
when you come second are your wife and your dog.

**DAMON HILL**

■■

New Yorkers love it when you spill your guts out
there [Flushing Meadow]. Spill your guts at Wimbledon
and they make you stop and clean it up.

**JIMMY CONNORS**

■■

Ladies, here's a hint; if you're playing against a friend who has big boobs, bring her to the net and make her hit backhand volleys. That's the hardest shot for the well-endowed. 'I've got to hit over them or under them, but I can't hit through,' Annie Jones used to always moan to me. Not having much in my bra, I found it hard to sympathize with her.

BILLIE JEAN KING, *THE AUTOBIOGRAPHY OF BILLIE JEAN KING*

Football's football; if that weren't the case,
it wouldn't be the game it is.

GARTH CROOKS

Swimming isn't a sport. It's just a way to keep from drowning.

GEORGE CARLIN

Boxers don't have sex before a fight.
Do you know why that is? They don't fancy each other.

JIMMY CARR

I'm not just involved in tennis, but committed.
Do you know the difference between involvement
and commitment? Think of ham and eggs. The chicken
is involved. The pig is committed.

MARTINA NAVRATILOVA

Last Saturday I watched a really cracking football match.
One of those matches you walk home from thinking,
'Yes, that is what soccer is all about.' Fourteen fouls in the
first ten minutes, fists flung, throats elbowed, eyes poked,
shins hacked, shirts ripped, hair pulled, enough ballistic
saliva to fill a trainer's bucket, and a richer variety of
air-blueing oaths, I'll wager, than Mary Whitehouse
has been able to net in a lifetime's trawling. Utterly
professional. Totally committed. Prodigiously physical.
Impressively cynical. Above all, unstintingly competitive,
and not a player on the field over twelve years old.

**ALAN COREN**

▪▪

And here's Moses Kiptanui – the nineteen-year-old Kenyan,
who turned twenty a few weeks ago.

**DAVID COLEMAN**

▪▪

Torvill and Dean, oh they're very good on ice. But you get
them out on the street . . . all over the place.

**HARRY HILL**

▪▪

Some people think football is a matter of life and death . . .
I can assure you it is much more serious than that.

**BILL SHANKLY, FORMER LIVERPOOL MANAGER**

▪▪

The centre forward said, 'It was an open goal –
but I put it straight over the crossbar! I could kick
myself!' And the manager said, 'I wouldn't bother,
you'd probably miss!'

**DAVID FROST**

■■

I cannot for the life of me see why the umpires, the
only two people on a cricket field who are not going
to get grass stains on their knees, are the only two people
allowed to wear dark trousers.

**KATHARINE WHITEHORN**

■■

We've lost seven of our last eight matches. The only team
that we have beaten is Western Samoa. It's a good job we
didn't play the whole of Samoa!

**GARETH DAVIES**

■■

For women, shopping is a sport; much like deer hunting
is to men. They are building a new mall in my town.
Last week, women were hanging on the fence yelling at the
workmen for taking a lunch break.

**JEFF FOXWORTHY**

■■

# YOU KNOW YOU'RE
# GETTING OLD WHEN...

You know you're getting old when all the names
in your black book have M.D. after them.

**HARRISON FORD**

▪

My parents didn't want to move to Florida,
but they turned sixty, and that's the law.

**JERRY SEINFELD**

▪

The University of Nebraska says that elderly people
that drink beer or wine at least four times a week have
the highest bone density. They need it – they're the ones
falling down the most.

**JAY LENO**

▪

If you live to be ninety in England and can still eat a
boiled egg, they think you deserve the Nobel Prize.

**ALAN BENNETT**

▪

I'm sixty-three now, but that's just seventeen Celsius.

**GEORGE CARLIN**

■■

At my age I do what Mark Twain did. I get my daily paper, look at the obituaries page and if I'm not there I carry on as usual.

**PATRICK MOORE**

■■

Sex at age ninety is like trying to shoot pool with a rope.

**GEORGE BURNS**

■■

Why on earth do people say things like, 'My eyes aren't what they used to be?' So what did they used to be? Ears? Wellington boots?

**BILLY CONNOLLY**

■■

Old age hangs on you like an old overcoat.

**QUENTIN CRISP**

■■

I'm at the age where my back goes out more than I do.

**PHYLLIS DILLER**

■■

My nan, she gets things mixed up, bless her. She gets the telephone mixed up with the hairdryer. You might have seen her around – wet hair, chapped lips.

**HARRY HILL**

My nan, she gets things mixed up, bless her. She gets the

I have the body of an eighteen year old.
I keep it in the fridge.

**SPIKE MILLIGAN**

Bored? Here's a way the over-fifty can easily kill off a good half-hour: Place your car keys in your right hand.
With your left hand, call a friend and confirm a lunch or dinner date. Hang up the phone. Now look for your car keys.

**STEVE MARTIN, *PURE DRIVEL***

My dad's pants kept creeping up on him. By sixty-five he was just a pair of pants and a head.

**JEFF ALTMAN**

I don't need you to remind me of my age.
I have a bladder to do that for me.

**STEPHEN FRY**

I don't feel eighty. In fact I don't feel anything
till noon. Then it's time for my nap.

BOB HOPE

I said to my husband, 'My boobs have gone, my
stomach's gone, say something nice about my legs.'
He said, 'Blue goes with everything.'

JOAN RIVERS

You know you're getting old when you get that one candle
on the cake. It's like, 'See if you can blow this out.'

JERRY SEINFELD

Life begins at forty – but so do fallen arches,
rheumatism, faulty eyesight, and the tendency to tell
a story to the same person three or four times.

HELEN ROWLAND

At my age, I don't even buy green bananas.

GEORGE BURNS

I can still enjoy sex at 74 – I live at 76 so it's no distance.

BOB MONKHOUSE

I knew I was going bald when it was taking longer
and longer to wash my face.

**HARRY HILL**

That phrase they use, 'in living memory' – as in 'the worst
floods in living memory' or 'the coldest winter in living
memory' – just how far back does it stretch because at my
age my 'living memory' goes back to a week last Tuesday.

**ALAN COREN**

Spare a thought for my friend Eliza Hamilton, who
was wrongly diagnosed as mentally unstable when
all she was, was a bit giddy.

**CAROLINE AHERNE, *THE MRS MERTON SHOW***

I'm at that age now where just putting my
cigar in its holder is a thrill.

**GEORGE BURNS**

If they offered me a knighthood, it would have to
be soon, while I can still get up from a kneeling
position within an hour.

**ROY HUDD**

As you get older, you've probably noticed that you tend to forget things. You'll be talking at a party, and you'll know that you know this person, but no matter how hard you try, you can't remember his or her name. This can be very embarrassing, especially if he or she turns out to be your spouse.

DAVE BARRY

■■

You know you're getting old when you're dashing through Marks & Spencer's, spot a pair of Dr Scholl's sandals, stop, and think, hmm, they look comfy.

VICTORIA WOOD

■■

# SELF-ABUSE

Reality is just a crutch for people who can't cope with drugs.

**ROBIN WILLIAMS**

I've joined Alcoholics Anonymous. I still drink,
but under a different name.

**JERRY DENNIS**

Smoking kills. If you're killed, you've lost a
very important part of your life.

**BROOKE SHIELDS**

I meant to address important questions such as:
When is it appropriate to get drunk? (When you're sober.)
When is it appropriate to sober up? (When you come to and
find your dog is wearing a negligee.)
Are there things you shouldn't say after letting go of the
water wagons with hands? ('I do.')

**P. J. O'ROURKE**

I quit smoking. I feel better, I smell better and it's safer to drink from old beer cans around the house.

ROSEANNE BARR

⊞

I've been smoking for thirty years now and there's nothing wrong with my lung.

FREDDIE STARR

⊞

I hate people who think it's clever to take drugs . . . like customs officers.

JACK DEE

⊞

I would never do crack . . . I would never do a drug named after a part of my ass, okay?

DENIS LEARY

⊞

We all know smoking is bad. I know I'm going to quit someday; if I thought I wasn't I'd quit now.

DYLAN MORAN

⊞

Cocaine is God's way of saying you're making too much money.

ROBIN WILLIAMS

⊞

I try to keep fit. I've got these parallel bars at home.
I run at them and try to buy a drink from both of them.

**ARTHUR SMITH**

■■

They're selling crack in my neighbourhood.
Finally.

**KEVIN BRENNAN**

■■

He once had his toes amputated so he could
stand closer to the bar.

**MIKE HARDING**

■■

I was so stoned in college that when my mom
would call I would still keep smoking out of my bong.
She'd hear the bubbles and say, 'What's going on
over there – are you sinking?'

**SCOTT SILVERMAN**

■■

I've never had any problem with drugs,
only policemen.

**KEITH RICHARDS**

■■

I'm not really a heavy smoker any more.
I only get through two lighters a day now.

**BILL HICKS**

I've stopped smoking . . . I think the cost was
a lot of it, and not being able to breathe. I first gave up
smoking when I was eight.

**DAVE ALLEN**

I used to have a drug problem, but now
I make enough money.

**DAVID LEE ROTH**

I did drugs to keep going. But performing in
itself is a drug. And taking cocaine is like being
a haemophiliac in a razor factory.

**ROBIN WILLIAMS**

# SELF-DEPRECATION

I wouldn't describe myself as a master of anything.

**TOBY YOUNG**

■■

My only claim to literary fame is that I used to deliver meat
to a woman who became T. S. Eliot's mother-in-law.

**ALAN BENNETT**

■■

I bear no grudges. I have a mind that retains nothing.

**BETTE MIDLER**

■■

People walk past me in the street and look at me,
but because they think I work in their office and
they can't remember my name.

**DYLAN MORAN**

■■

When you finally accept that you're a complete dork,
your life gets easier. No sense in trying to be cool.

**REESE WITHERSPOON**

■■

I find it rather easy to portray a businessman. Being bland, rather cruel and incompetent comes naturally to me.

JOHN CLEESE

I don't think I've got bad taste. I've got no taste.

GRAHAM NORTON

I enjoy using the comedy technique of self-deprecation – but I'm not very good at it.

ARNOLD BROWN

The most horrific thing that happened was that I was photographed with my shirt off and I was fat. Can you imagine two worse things than being fat and gay?

GEORGE MICHAEL ON HIS ARREST

I once made love for an hour and fifteen minutes, but it was the night the clocks are set ahead.

GARRY SHANDLING

The fashion world don't trust me anymore. And why should they? I looked crap for years.

COURTNEY LOVE

If my film makes one more person miserable,
I've done my job.

**WOODY ALLEN**

■■

Homer Simpson: How is education supposed to make
me feel smarter? Besides, every time I learn something
new, it pushes some old stuff out of my brain.
Remember when I took that home winemaking course,
and I forgot how to drive?

**GREG DANIELS, WRITER, *THE SIMPSONS***

■■

If you had seen me in my teens you would have
bolted for the door without picking up your coat.

**JOANNA LUMLEY**

■■

When I appear in public, people expect me to neigh,
grind my teeth, paw the ground and swish my tail –
none of which is easy.

**PRINCESS ANNE**

■■

When I was a child, I was so fat I was the one chosen
to play Bethlehem in the school nativity play.

**JO BRAND**

■■

I wanted to be a comedian because I was heavy
and I knew a lot of fat comics.

BRYAN MCFADDEN

▪▪

I used to think I was an interesting person, but
I must tell you how sobering a thought it is to realize
your life's story fills about thirty-five pages and you
have, actually, not much to say.

ROSEANNE BARR

▪▪

I never know how much of what I say is true.

BETTE MIDLER, *A VIEW FROM A BROAD*

▪▪

I feel for eight minutes on screen, I should
only get a little bit.

JUDI DENCH ON ACCEPTING HER OSCAR
FOR *SHAKESPEARE IN LOVE*

▪▪

My career must be slipping. This is the first
time I've been available to pick up an award.

MICHAEL CAINE

▪▪

Despite massive discouragement, I remain myself.
Somebody has to be me, so it might as well be me.

**MORRISSEY**

■■

They laughed when I said I was going to be a
comedian . . . They're not laughing now.

**BOB MONKHOUSE**

■■

Nine months of listening to the Rolling Stones is
not my idea of heaven.

**MICK JAGGER, HAVING FINISHED RECORDING THE
ALBUM *LOVE YOU LIVE***

■■

I'm not a fighter, I have bad reflexes.
I was once run over by a car being pushed by two guys.

**WOODY ALLEN**

■■

I have to struggle not to be the most obstreperous
member of the audience at my own plays, in the
meantime scowling murderously at anyone who as
much as adjusts a buttock or pats a partner's knee.

**SIMON GRAY, *FAT CHANCE***

■■

I wouldn't change anything, but I could do with sharing
my bottom and thighs with at least two other people.

CHRISTINE HAMILTON

■■

I feel like I'm not smart enough to answer the questions
I'm asked.

BRET EASTON ELLIS

■■

I cannot sing, dance or act; what else would
I be but a talk-show host.

DAVID LETTERMAN

■■

I have low self-esteem. When we were in bed together,
I would fantasize that *I* was someone else.

RICHARD LEWIS

■■

I am afraid it is a non-starter.
I cannot even use a bicycle pump.

JUDI DENCH ON USING THE INTERNET

■■

I always get the feeling that when lesbians are looking at me,
they're thinking, 'That's why I'm not a heterosexual.'

GEORGE COSTANZA (JASON ALEXANDER), *SEINFELD*

■■

# HOME TRUTHS

A cousin of mine who was a casualty surgeon in
Manhattan tells me that he and his colleagues had
a one-word nickname for bikers: donors.

STEPHEN FRY, *PAPERWEIGHT*

▪▪

They lie about marijuana. Tell you pot-smoking makes
you unmotivated. Lie! When you're high, you can do
everything you normally do just as well. You just realize
that it's not worth the fucking effort.

BILL HICKS

▪▪

As we head to war with Iraq, President Bush
wants to make one thing clear:
this war is not about oil, it's about gasoline.

JAY LENO

▪▪

One of the most awkward things that can
happen in a pub is when your pint-to-toilet cycle gets
synchronized with a complete stranger.

PETER KAY

▪▪

Oxymoron is a literary device whereby two contradictory concepts are juxtaposed: as, for example, in 'the witty Jane Austen'.

PATRICK MURRAY

■■

Science has conquered many diseases, broken the genetic code and even placed human beings on the moon, yet when a man of eighty is left in a room with two eighteen-year-old cocktail waitresses, nothing happens. Because the real problems never change.

WOODY ALLEN

■■

It seems so lazy to have an affair with your secretary, like always going to the nearest restaurant instead of the best.

LYNN BARBER

■■

The great advantage of being in a rut is that when one is in a rut, one knows exactly where one is.

ALAN BENNETT

■■

If it's the Psychic Network, why do they need a phone number?

ROBIN WILLIAMS

■■

It's amazing what you can do with an E in A-level Art, twisted imagination and a chainsaw.

**DAMIEN HIRST**

■■

Here is the truth about *Titanic: people wanted to see it.* Here is the truth about *The Postman: people didn't want to see it.* Everything else is mythology.

**WILLIAM GOLDMAN, *WHICH LIE DID I TELL?***

■■

Hypochondria is Greek for 'men'.

**KATHY LETTE**

■■

There is no such thing as fun for the whole family.

**JERRY SEINFELD**

■■

Many journalists have fallen for the conspiracy theory of government. I do assure you that they would produce more accurate work if they adhered to the cock-up theory.

**BERNARD INGHAM**

■■

There is a very fine line between 'hobby' and 'mental illness'.

**DAVE BARRY**

■■

Recession is when your neighbour loses his job.
Depression is when you lose yours.
And recovery is when Jimmy Carter loses his.

RONALD REAGAN DURING THE 1980 PRESIDENTIAL CAMPAIGN

Love, marriage and kids are fine, but I wouldn't
give up an hour of comedy for them.

FRANK SKINNER

The first law of the shower states that no two shower
controls in the universe are the same. The second states
that the temperature markings on shower controls bear
no relation to the temperature of the water. The third
states that, however much a shower control may rotate, the
degree of rotation required to change from ice-cold to
scalding is never more than one millimetre.

JOE BENNETT, *FUN RUN AND OTHER OXYMORONS*

Accent is the snake and the ladder in the upstairs
downstairs of social ambition.

MELVYN BRAGG

Men who listen to classical music tend not to spit.

RITA RUDNER

The very first law in advertising is to avoid the concrete
promise and cultivate the delightfully vague.

BILL COSBY

██

I see TV ads about detergents that can get bloodstains out of
your clothes. I say if you have bloodstains on your clothes
you should be thinking about something other than laundry.

JERRY SEINFELD

██

Sequels are whores' movies.

WILLIAM GOLDMAN, *WHICH LIE DID I TELL?*

██

Honesty may be the best policy, but it's important
to remember that apparently, by elimination,
dishonesty is the second-best policy.

GEORGE CARLIN

██

Nobody ever dares make Cup-a-Soup in a bowl.

PETER KAY

██

The marvellous thing about a joke with a double
meaning is that it can only mean one thing.

RONNIE BARKER

██

There is, perhaps, no more dangerous man in the world than the man with the sensibilities of an artist but without creative talent. With luck such men make wonderful theatrical impresarios and interior decorators, or else they become mass murderers or critics.

**BARRY HUMPHRIES, *MORE PLEASE***

Men, we drive ourselves crazy. Men always want to marry a virgin, but during the act of sex on the wedding night we tell the women to say 'You're the best, you're the best', then afterwards we wonder, better than who?

**JERRY SEINFELD**

You've turned into your dad the day you put aside a thin piece of wood specifically to stir paint with.

**PETER KAY**

Get a job, your husband hates you. Get a good job, your husband leaves you. Get a stupendous job, your husband leaves you for a teenager.

**CYNTHIA HEIMEL, *IF YOU CAN'T LIVE WITHOUT ME, WHY AREN'T YOU DEAD YET?***

The useless piece of flesh at the end of a penis is a man.

**JO BRAND**

■■

The only good thing about leotards is that they're
a very effective deterrent against any sort of unwanted
attention. If you're wearing stretch knickers, stretch tights,
and a stretch Lycra leotard, you might as well try and
sexually harass a trampoline.

**VICTORIA WOOD**

■■

A computer is a stupid machine with the ability to do
incredibly smart things, while computer programmers are
smart people with the ability to do incredibly stupid things.

**BILL BRYSON,** *I'M A STRANGER HERE MYSELF*

■■

I think that women just have a primeval instinct
to make soup, which they will try to foist on anybody
who looks like a likely candidate.

**DYLAN MORAN**

■■

I go to the theatre to be entertained. I don't want to
see rape, sodomy, incest and drug addiction.
I can get all of that at home.

**PETER COOK**

■■

# ON BEING A SUPERSTAR

When someone follows you all the way to the shop and watches you buy toilet roll, you know your life has changed.

JENNIFER ANISTON

❖❖

I didn't like being a celebrity. It's like a service job.
Like washing toilets.

BJÖRK

❖❖

I think we've gorged on celebrity and we're soon going to be sick. And I'll probably be one of the first to be vomited out.

MELINDA MESSENGER

❖❖

The social habits of famous people are like the
sexual practices of porcupines, which urinate on each
other to soften the quills.

P. J. O'ROURKE, *MODERN MANNERS*

❖❖

Anyone who thinks my story is anywhere
near over is sadly mistaken.

DONALD TRUMP

❖❖

Slowly but surely, what was once something that you would never do, first becomes the thing you're using to get something else, and then suddenly it's what you are doing. Next week.

RUPERT EVERETT, *RED CARPETS AND OTHER BANANA SKINS*

▪▪

Fame is being asked to sign your autograph on the back of a cigarette packet.

BILLY CONNOLLY

▪▪

Imagine their delighted surprise when I read them the script of *Love and Death*, with its plot that went from war to political assassination, ending with the death of its hero caused by a cruel trick of God. Never having witnessed eight film executives go into cardiac arrest simultaneously, I was quite amused.

WOODY ALLEN

▪▪

I don't like this reality television, I have to be honest . . . I think real people should not be on television. It's for special people like us, people who have trained and studied to appear to be real.

GARRY SHANDLING

▪▪

I don't use any particular method. I'm from the
let's pretend school of acting.

HARRISON FORD

A very quiet and tasteful way to be famous is to
have a famous relation. Then you can not only be nothing,
you can do nothing too.

P. J. O'ROURKE, *MODERN MANNERS*

Steven Spielberg is so powerful he had final
cut at his own circumcision.

ROBIN WILLIAMS

The missus says that if someone in the street doesn't
recognize me, I go back and tell them who I am.

RON ATKINSON

I am always delighted to see Ms [Vanessa] Feltz on
my television because the sight always convinces me that
I was wise to invest in a widescreen set.

VICTOR LEWIS-SMITH

Being stared at is not fun . . . There are times when
someone on the street says, 'Are you William Hurt?'
and I will say, 'No, not at the moment.'

**WILLIAM HURT, *SUNDAY TELEGRAPH*, 2000**

The only people who are desperate to go on the show
are people we're desperate not to have on the show.

**GRAHAM NORTON**

Actors say they do their own stunts for the integrity of the
film, but I did them because they looked like a lot of fun.

**STEVE COOGAN**

I'm not very wild. I tried to trash hotel rooms when I was
younger, but I just ended up making the bed and leaving a
small chocolate on the pillow for the maid.

**ARDAL O'HANLON**

It's hard to be naked in a scene and not be
upstaged by your nipples.

**SUSAN SARANDON**

I didn't even know my bra size
until I made a movie.

ANGELINA JOLIE

⬚

He longed for an audience, the prospect
of which terrified him.

SIMON GRAY ON STEPHEN FRY, *FAT CHANCE*

⬚

I go in and out of fashion like a
double-breasted suit.

ALAN AYCKBOURN

⬚

# MORE STARS AND A FEW STRIPES

I come from a part of the world where the
Egg McMuffin would be a heritage object.

**BILL BRYSON**

■■

The problem with Yanks is they are wimps.

**GORDON RAMSAY**

■■

I like America to some extent.

**MICHAEL MOORE**

■■

Europeans think Americans are fat, vulgar, greedy, stupid,
ambitious and ignorant, and so on. And they've taken as their
own, as their representative American, someone who actually
embodies all of those qualities.

**CHRISTOPHER HITCHENS ON MICHAEL MOORE**

■■

The American language is in a state of flux
based on the survival of the unfittest.

**CYRIL CONNOLLY, *SUNDAY TIMES*, 1996**

■■

Whoever invented the meeting must have had Hollywood in mind. I think they should consider giving Oscars for meetings. Best Meeting of the Year, Best Supporting Meeting, Best Meeting Based on Material from Another Meeting.

WILLIAM GOLDMAN, *ADVENTURES IN THE SCREEN TRADE*

■■

Whatever it is that the government does, sensible Americans would prefer that the government does it to somebody else. This is the idea behind foreign policy.

P. J. O'ROURKE, *PARLIAMENT OF WHORES*

■■

Ninety-nine per cent of the adults in this country are decent, hard-working, honest Americans. It's the other lousy one per cent that gets all the publicity and gives us a bad name. But then, we elected them.

LILY TOMLIN

■■

The average Southerner has the speech patterns of someone slipping in and out of consciousness. I can change my shoes and socks faster than most people in Mississippi can speak a sentence.

BILL BRYSON

■■

America is a vast conspiracy to make you happy.

JOHN UPDIKE, *PROBLEMS*

■■

Hollywood is Disneyland staged by Dante.
You imagine purgatory is like this, except that the
parking is not so good.

**ROBIN WILLIAMS**

When an American heiress wants to buy a man, she at once
crosses the Atlantic. The only really materialistic people I
have met have been Europeans.

**MARY McCARTHY**

America is our neighbour, our ally, our trading partner,
and our friend. Still, sometimes you'd like to give
them such a smack . . .

**RICK MERCER**

We live in a country where John Lennon takes six bullets in
the chest. Yoko Ono is standing right next to him. Not one
f**king bullet. Explain that to me! Explain that to me!

**DENIS LEARY**

Americans have different ways of saying things. They say
'elevator', we say 'lift'. They say 'President', we say, 'stupid
psychopathic git.'

**ALEXEI SAYLE**

America is a melting pot; the people at the bottom get
burned while all the scum floats to the top.

**CHARLIE KING**

■■

Americans who travel abroad for the first time are often
shocked to discover that, despite all the progress that has
been made in the last thirty years, many foreign people still
speak in foreign languages.

**DAVE BARRY**

■■

In America, everything goes and nothing matters, while in
Europe, nothing goes and everything matters.

**PHILIP ROTH**

■■

He's not Hollywood. He doesn't read synopses –
he reads the entire text.

**ROBERT EVANS, *THE KID STAYS IN THE PICTURE***

■■

I visited an American supermarket. They have so many
amazing products here. Like powder milk. You add water and
you get milk. And powder orange juice. You add water and
you get orange juice. Then I saw baby powder. And I said to
myself, 'What a country! I'm making my family tonight!'

**YAKOV SMIRNOFF**

■■

# FILTHY LUCRE

Money – the one thing that keeps us
in touch with our children.

**GYLES BRANDRETH**

∷

Normal is getting dressed in clothes that you buy for work
and driving through traffic in a car that you are still paying
for – in order to get to the job you need to pay for the
clothes and the car, and the house you leave vacant all day
so you can afford to live in it.

**ELLEN DEGENERES**

∷

Having money is rather like being a blonde.
It is more fun but not vital.

**MARY QUANT**

∷

All right, so I like spending money!
But name one other extravagance!

**MAX KAUFFMANN**

∷

A guy told me, 'To a farmer manure smells like money.'
I said, 'Maybe he should start keeping his wallet in his
front pocket.'

**TAMMY PATORELLI**

❊

I haven't reported my missing credit card to the police
because whoever stole it is spending less than my wife.

**ILIE NASTASE**

❊

The great rule is not to talk about money with people
who have much more or much less than you.

**KATHARINE WHITEHORN**

❊

I told the Inland Revenue I didn't owe them a penny
because I lived near the sea.

**KEN DODD**

❊

It's your money. You paid for it.

**GEORGE W. BUSH**

❊

The buck stops with the guy who signs the cheques.

**RUPERT MURDOCH**

❊

# FILTHY LUCRE

It's true that nothing is certain except death and taxes.
Sometimes I wish they came in that order.

SAM LEVENSON

■■

I'm a millionaire, I'm a multi-millionaire. I'm filthy rich.
You know why I'm a multi-millionaire?
'Cause multi-millions like what I do.

MICHAEL MOORE

■■

What first, Debbie, attracted you to the
millionaire Paul Daniels?

CAROLINE AHERNE, *THE MRS MERTON SHOW*

■■

All I ask is the chance to prove that
money can't make me happy.

SPIKE MILLIGAN

■■

I get so tired of listening to one million dollars
here, one million dollars there. It's so petty.

IMELDA MARCOS

■■

It's better to spend money like there's no tomorrow
than to spend tonight like there's no money.

P. J. O'ROURKE, *MODERN MANNERS*

###

A bank is a place that will lend you money if
you can prove you don't need it.

BOB HOPE

###

They usually have two tellers in my local bank,
except when it's very busy, when they have one.

RITA RUDNER

###

I have enough money to last me the rest of my
life unless I buy something.

JACKIE MASON, *JACKIE MASON'S AMERICA*

###

I'm the fall guy – I only blew £200m.

NICK LEESON, DERIVATIVES TRADER WHO LOST
BARINGS BANK £827M IN 1995

###

It's clearly a budget. It's got a lot of numbers in it.

GEORGE W. BUSH

###

I've written books on advertising . . .
cheque books.

**ALAN SUGAR**

■■

Bill Gates made a pact with the Devil.
The Devil said, 'You can have $100 billion,
but you have to go through life looking like a turtle.'

**DANA CARVEY**

■■

# HOME AND AWAY

England is the only country where food
is more dangerous than sex.

JACKIE MASON, *THE WORLD ACCORDING TO ME*

■■

The English like eccentrics. They just don't
like them living next door.

JULIAN CLARY

■■

A soggy little island huffing and puffing to
keep up with Western Europe.

JOHN UPDIKE ON ENGLAND, *PICKED UP PIECES*

■■

Whenever I talk about running the Sporting Relief mile with
Prince William, I say that was a great day till I had to go
back to Belfast and explain what I'd become. I'm a Brit-loving,
arse-kissing, stooping, two-faced bastard. Straight red card.

PATRICK KIELTY

■■

Boy, those French, they have a different word for everything.

STEVE MARTIN

■■

The only thing they [the English] have ever done for
European agriculture is mad cow disease.

**JACQUES CHIRAC**

::

Let's be frank, the Italians' technological contribution
to humankind stopped with the pizza oven.

**BILL BRYSON, *NEITHER HERE NOR THERE***

::

You can always reason with a German. You can always
reason with a barnyard animal, too, for all the good it does.

**P. J. O'ROURKE, *HOLIDAYS IN HELL***

::

The English are obsessed with class. Even your letters travel
first and second class. Do the first-class letters get a little
in-flight movie and paper-parasoled cocktail en route?

**KATHY LETTE**

::

Australians go to work in shorts and that's a
good enough reason to hate them.

**JEREMY CLARKSON**

::

The airport staff resemble leftover recruits from the Luftwaffe, with attitude: that FUCK YOU look that transmits messages to your legs to U-turn and bound back into the aircraft. No one seems used to the idea yet that people can enter and leave of their own volition.

**RICHARD E. GRANT ON HUNGARY, *WITH NAILS***

❖

To live in Australia permanently is rather like going to a party and dancing all night with your mother.

**BARRY HUMPHRIES**

❖

I think Australians like a bit of vulgarity.

**JULIAN CLARY**

❖

A lot of my countrymen say rude things about England because it has the lowest standard of living in the world, and I don't think that's fair. I think that's mean and horrid. Because I know England will rise again. It will – say, to the level of Sicily or Ethiopia.

**DAME EDNA EVERAGE (BARRY HUMPHRIES)**

❖

Listen, I would call the French scumbags, but that, of course, would be a disservice to bags filled with scum.

**DENNIS MILLER**

❖

Geographically, Ireland is a medium-sized rural island
that is slowly but steadily being consumed by sheep.

**DAVE BARRY**

■■

The British tourist is always happy abroad as
long as the natives are waiters.

**ROBERT MORLEY**

■■

I think we should take Iraq and Iran and combine
them into one country and call it Irate.
All the pissed-off people live in one
place and get it over with.

**DENIS LEARY**

■■

Canada is an entire country named Doug.

**GREG PROOPS**

■■

Australia is a huge rest home, where no unwelcome
news is ever wafted on to the pages of the worst
newspapers in the world.

**GERMAINE GREER**

■■

Ernie: Didn't you know any Spanish?
Eric: I knew two words and they reckon that's all you
need to know for honeymooning in Spain.
Ernie: And what are they?
Eric: 'Manana' – that means 'Tonight'. And 'Pyjama' –
that means 'Tonight'.

ERIC MORECAMBE AND ERNIE WISE,
*THE MORECAMBE AND WISE JOKE BOOK*

▪▪

A broad school of Australian writing has based itself on the
assumption that Australia not only has a history worth
bothering about, but that all the history worth bothering
about happened in Australia.

CLIVE JAMES, *THE DREAMING SWIMMER*

▪▪

There have been many definitions of hell, but for the English
the best definition is that it is the place where the Germans
are the police, the Swedish are the comedians, the Italians
are the defence force, the Frenchmen dig the roads, the
Belgians are the pop singers, the Spanish run the railways, the
Turks cook the food, the Irish are the waiters, the Greeks run
the government, and the common language is Dutch.

DAVID FROST AND ANTONY JAY

▪▪

When it's three o'clock in New York, it's still 1938 in London.

BETTE MIDLER

▪▪

German is the most extravagantly ugly language.
It sounds like someone using a sick bag on a 747.

**WILLIAM RUSHTON**

██

The American dream is that any citizen can rise to the
highest office in the land. The British Dream is that the
Queen drops in for tea.

**MICHAEL BYWATER**

██

Never shoot a film in Belgrade, Yugoslavia! The whole town
is illuminated by a 20-watt night light and there's nothing to
do. You can't even go for a drive. Tito is always using the car.

**MEL BROOKS**

██

*Racial Characteristics* of the Scottish: sour, stingy, depressing
beggars who parade around in schoolgirls' skirts with
nothing on underneath. Their fumbled attempt at speaking
the English language has been a source of amusement for five
centuries, and their idiot music has been dreaded by those
not blessed with deafness for at least as long.

**P. J. O'ROURKE, 'FOREIGNERS AROUND THE
WORLD', *NATIONAL LAMPOON*, 1976**

██

The food in Yugoslavia is fine if you like pork tartare.

**ED BEGLEY JNR**

██

Norwegian charisma is somewhere between a
Presbyterian minister and a tree.

JOHNNY CARSON

In France, they're having trouble translating a lot of Internet
terms into French. In France, the law is you have to use
French words. For example, there are no French words for
'surfing the Web', there aren't any French words for 'chat
session', and there aren't any French words for 'hacker'.
Of course, a lot of other words don't translate to French
either: military victory, deodorant . . .

JAY LENO

In Russia, show the least athletic aptitude and
they've got you dangling off the parallel bars with
a leotard full of hormones.

VICTORIA WOOD

Belgium has only one real claim to fame. Thanks to all
the wars that have been fought on its soil, there are
more dead people there than anywhere else in the world.
So, while there's no quality of life in Belgium, there is a
simply wonderful quality of death.

JEREMY CLARKSON

# THE PROFESSIONALS

Patient: Are you the gynaecologist?
Gynaecologist: At your cervix, madam!
Patient: Dilated to meet you!

**ANONYMOUS**

�֍

I was under the care of a couple of medical students
who couldn't diagnose a decapitation.

**JEFFREY BERNARD**

✖

You know it's time to start using mouthwash when
your dentist leaves the room and sends in a canary.

**JOAN RIVERS**

✖

First the doctor told me the good news.
I was going to have a disease named after me.

**STEVE MARTIN**

✖

Who is your career counsellor? Icarus?

**JOHN GOLDSMITH TO A LAWYER NOTED FOR FIRING HIS CLIENTS**

✖

Ernie: Doctor, I don't know what's wrong with me.
Do you think I'll ever get better?
Eric: I don't know – let me feel your purse.
Ernie: But, Doctor . . .
Eric: Sit down and tell me about it . . .
Ernie: Doctor, I'm not a private patient.
I'm on the National Health.
Eric: . . . in less than two minutes.

**ERIC MORECAMBE AND ERNIE WISE,**
*THE MORECAMBE AND WISE JOKE BOOK*

■

One of the things I like most about lawyers is the
big shock absorber they have strapped to their brains.
Put it this way, if a lawyer's ego was hit by lightning,
the lightning would be hospitalized.

**KATHY LETTE**

■

A woman went to a plastic surgeon and asked him to
make her like Bo Derek. He gave her a lobotomy.

**JOAN RIVERS**

■

An apple a day keeps the doctor away.
So does not having health insurance.

**JOE HICKMAN**

■

After a year in therapy, my psychiatrist said to me,
'Maybe life isn't for everyone.'

**LARRY BROWN**

∷

I'm always amazed to hear of air-crash victims so badly
mutilated that they have to be identified by their dental
records. What I can't understand is, if they don't know who
you are, how do they know who your dentist is?

**PAUL MERTON**

∷

My psychiatrist told me I was crazy and I said I want
a second opinion. He said, 'Okay, you're ugly too.'

**RODNEY DANGERFIELD**

∷

I hate the waiting room. Because it's called the waiting room,
there's no chance of not waiting. It's built, designed and
intended for waiting. Why would they take you right away
when they've got this room all set up?

**JERRY SEINFELD**

∷

Happiness is your dentist telling you it won't hurt
and then having him catch his hand in the drill.

**JOHNNY CARSON**

∷

Estate agents. You can't live with them, you can't live with them. The first sign of these nasty purulent sores appeared round about 1894. With their jangling keys, nasty suits, revolting beards, moustaches and tinted spectacles, estate agents roam the land causing perturbation and despair. If you try and kill them, you're put in prison: if you try and talk to them, you vomit. There's only one thing worse than an estate agent, but at least that can be safely lanced, drained and surgically dressed. Estate agents. Love them or loathe them, you'd be mad not to loathe them.

STEPHEN FRY

Never go to a doctor whose office plants have died.

ERMA BOMBECK

We do have a zeal for laughter in most situations, give or take a dentist.

JOSEPH HELLER

I busted a mirror and got seven years bad luck, but my lawyer thinks he can get me five.

STEVEN WRIGHT

My parents wanted me to be a lawyer.
But I don't think I would have been very happy.
I'd be in front of the jury singing.

**JENNIFER LOPEZ**

■■

I saw a specialist who asked me, 'Are you familiar
with the phrase "faecal impaction"?' I said, 'I think I saw
that one with Glenn Close and Michael Douglas.'

**BOB MONKHOUSE**

■■

A psychiatrist is a man who goes to a strip club
and watches the audience.

**MERV STOCKWOOD**

■■

I went to the dentist. He said, 'Say aaah.' I said,
'Why?' He said, 'My dog's died.'

**TOMMY COOPER**

■■

The only difference between a dead skunk lying in the
road and a dead lawyer lying in the road is that there
are skid marks around the skunk.

**PATRICK MURRAY**

■■

# SMALL PEOPLE

If worse comes to worst, there is no parenting tool
more powerful than a good hug. If you sense that your
child is getting into trouble, you must give that child a great
big fat hug in a public place with other young people around,
while saying, in a loud piercing voice, 'You are MY LITTLE
BABY and I love you NO MATTER WHAT!'
This will embarrass your child so much that he or she
may immediately run off and join a strict religious order
whose entire diet consists of gravel. If one hug doesn't
work, threaten to give your child another.

**DAVE BARRY**

▪▪

A two-year-old is like having a blender,
but you don't have a top for it.

**JERRY SEINFELD**

▪▪

I'm trying to decide whether or not to have children.
My time is running out. I know I want to have
children while my parents are still young enough to
take care of them.

**RITA RUDNER**

▪▪

Experts say you should never hit your children in anger.
When is a good time? When you're feeling festive?

**ROSEANNE BARR**

My first rule of consumerism is never to buy anything
you can't make your children carry.

**BILL BRYSON**

I love to go to the playground and watch the children
jumping up and down. They don't know I'm firing blanks.

**EMO PHILIPS**

We've begun to long for the pitter-patter of little feet.
So we bought a dog. Well, it's cheaper and you get more feet.

**RITA RUDNER**

Do not allow children to mix drinks. It is unseemly
and they use too much vermouth.

**STEVE ALLEN**

She was growing up, and that was the direction I wanted
her to take. Who wants a daughter that grows sideways?

**SPIKE MILLIGAN**

Always end the name of your child with a vowel
so that when you yell the name will carry.

**BILL COSBY**

On my first day at school, my parents dropped me off at the
wrong nursery. There I was surrounded by trees and bushes.

**KEN DODD**

People who are pro smacking children say,
'It's the only language they understand.'
You could apply that to tourists.

**JACK DEE**

I'm in that benign form of house arrest
that is looking after a baby.

**J. K. ROWLING**

Everyone should have kids. They are the greatest joy
in the world. But they are also terrorists.
You'll realize this as soon as they are born, and they start
using sleep deprivation to break you.

**RAY ROMANO**

Why do parents always take their children to
supermarkets to smack them?

**JACK DEE**

■■

You don't appreciate a lot of stuff in school until you get
older. Little things like being spanked every day by a middle-
aged woman – stuff you pay good money for in later life.

**EMO PHILIPS**

■■

Make no mistake about why these babies are here –
they are here to replace us.

**JERRY SEINFELD**

■■

Kids, they are always hurting themselves. It's like,
'Quick, get me to casualty quick!' while you're doing
something important like sitting down picking your ear.

**DYLAN MORAN**

■■

Babies don't need a vacation but I still see them at
the beach. I'll go over to them and say, 'What are you doing
here, you've never worked a day in your life!'

**STEVEN WRIGHT**

■■

Kids are wonderful, but I like mine barbecued.

**BOB HOPE**

I've spent two years being politically correct about parents,
but it's time to say, if you're giving your young kids fizzy
drinks then you're an arsehole and a tosser.

**JAMIE OLIVER**

I understand the importance of
bondage between parent and child.

**DAN QUAYLE**

I don't believe in smacking children –
I just use a cattle prod.

**JENNY ECLAIR**

Sex education may be a good idea in the schools,
but I don't believe the kids should be given homework.

**BILL COSBY**

# KEEPING UP APPEARANCES

They should put expiration dates on clothing so
we men will know when they go out of style.

**GARRY SHANDLING**

■■

The media may believe I dress badly, but that's
not the opinion of the people.

**NANCY DELL'OLIO**

■■

I scramble into my clothes – whatever's lying in
a heap on the floor. I do, however, put on a clean
pair of underpants each morning – by Friday I've
got seven pairs on.

**PAMELA STEPHENSON**

■■

It is totally impossible to be well
dressed in cheap shoes.

**HARDY AMIES, *THE ENGLISHMAN'S SUIT***

■■

I have an *Alice in Wonderland* White Rabbit costume
in a wardrobe. I had it for a school play when I was nine.
I can't get into it now, but if I'm feeling very low, I
sometimes put on the polystyrene ears to watch TV.

HUGH GRANT

I have to be careful to get out before I become the grotesque
caricature of a hatchet-faced woman with big knockers.

JAMIE LEE CURTIS

Jews are the best dressers in the world. They buy the best
clothes, the best homes, the best cars. The best of everything.
The only thing is they get it for less.

JACKIE MASON

The most beautiful thing that I ever saw was a woman.
There are things that are second and third – the moon and
the sunsets, great mountains and lakes – but first, a woman.

LEONARD COHEN

When you buy a V-neck sweater there's a V of material
missing. You know what they do with that? They send it
to Ann Summers and she makes those fancy pants.

HARRY HILL

I was forty-nine when I posed for the cover of
*Playboy* magazine.
I looked good, so why not? As you age, you get the
face you deserve.

JOAN COLLINS

::

One of the few lessons I have learned in life is that
there is invariably something odd about women
who wear ankle socks.

ALAN BENNETT

::

Glasses can alter your personality completely –
if you empty them often enough.

JERRY DENNIS

::

I'm the female equivalent of a counterfeit $20 bill.
Half of what you see is a pretty good reproduction,
the rest is fraud.

CHER

::

I spent seven hours in a beauty shop –
and that was just for the estimate.

PHYLLIS DILLER

::

Frasier: I do not have a fat face!
Niles: Oh, please! I keep wondering how
long you're going to store those nuts for winter.

**DON SEIGEL AND JERRY PERZIGIAN, WRITERS, *FRASIER***

❊

The method preferred by most balding men for
making themselves look silly is called the 'comb-over',
which is when the man grows the hair on one side
of his head very long and combs it across the bald area,
creating an effect that looks from the top like an egg
in the grasp of a large tropical spider.

**DAVE BARRY**

❊

It wasn't a fortune. It cost me the price of
one and a half Hermès handbags.

**ANNE ROBINSON TALKING ABOUT HER COSMETIC SURGERY**

❊

If God had meant breasts to be lifted and separated,
he would have put one on each shoulder.

**VICTORIA WOOD**

❊

My physique is down to twenty years of eating cheese.

**RICKY GERVAIS**

❊

Clothes make the man. Naked people have
little or no influence in society.

**MARK TWAIN**

■■

It's not a beard, it's an animal
I've trained to sit very still.

**BILL BAILEY**

■■

My body is falling so fast, my gynaecologist wears a hard hat.

**JOAN RIVERS**

■■

I took my husband to the hospital yesterday to
have seventeen stitches out – that'll teach him to buy
me a sewing kit for my birthday.

**JO BRAND**

■■

I like having dyed hair and big teeth. Once you go
down the route of trying to look like a stereotypical babe,
you are doomed.

**JANET STREET-PORTER**

■■

I got some new underwear the other day. Well, new to me.

**EMO PHILIPS**

■■

Can young people wear their pants any lower?
Their waistbands are now at approximately knee level.
Where will this trend end? The shins? The feet?
Will young people eventually detach themselves from
their pants altogether and just drag them along behind,
connected to their ankles by a belt?

DAVE BARRY

I do not think if I had had a full head of hair,
there would have been a Tory landslide.

WILLIAM HAGUE

Fur is a subject that makes sensitive toes
curl in their leather shoes.

JEREMY PAXMAN

# DEATH

Pete: Have you ever thought about death?
Do you realize that we each must die?
Dud: Of course we must die, but not yet.
It's only half past four of a Wednesday afternoon.

PETER COOK AND DUDLEY MOORE,
*THE DAGENHAM DIALOGUES*

■■

I wanna live till I die, no more, no less.

EDDIE IZZARD

■■

In India, when a man dies his widow throws herself
on the funeral pyre. Over here, she says, 'Fifty ham baps,
Beryl – you slice, I'll butter.'

VICTORIA WOOD

■■

My aunt used to say, 'What you can't see,
can't hurt you' . . . well, she died of radiation
poisoning a few months back!

HARRY HILL

■■

The Chalk Outline guy's got a good job. Not too dangerous, the criminals are long gone. I guess these are people who wanted to be sketch artists, but they couldn't draw very well. 'Uh, listen, Jon, forget the sketches, do you think if we left the dead body right there on the sidewalk you could manage to trace around it?'

**JERRY SEINFELD**

Death is nature's way of saying,
'Your table's ready.'

**ROBIN WILLIAMS**

I bet Maurice Gibb's heart monitor was singing the tune of 'Stayin' Alive'.

**GRAHAM NORTON**

I'd hate to drown.
You look so awful afterwards.

**ALAN AYCKBOURN**

The key is to not think of death as an end, but as more of a very effective way to cut down on your expenses.

**WOODY ALLEN, *LOVE AND DEATH***

Alan died suddenly at Saltwood on Sunday 5th September.
He said he would like it to be stated that he regarded himself
as having gone to join Tom and the other dogs.

ANNOUNCEMENT IN *THE TIMES* OF ALAN CLARK'S DEATH,
8 SEPTEMBER 1999

If you die in an elevator, be sure
to push the 'Up' button.

SAM LEVENSON

Basil: If a guest isn't singing, 'Oh, What a Beautiful Morning'
I don't immediately think, 'Oh, there's another snuffed
it in the night. Another name in the Fawlty Towers Book
of Remembrance.' I mean this is a hotel, not the
Burma Railway.

JOHN CLEESE AND CONNIE BOOTH, WRITERS, *FAWLTY TOWERS*

I hope you die first as I don't want you singing at my funeral.

SPIKE MILLIGAN TO HARRY SECOMBE

People will be in a state of real shock.
There will be grief that you would not get for anyone else.

TONY BLAIR ON THE DEATH OF PRINCESS DIANA

It is sobering to consider that when Mozart was
my age he had already been dead for a year.

**TOM LEHRER**

Life was a funny thing that happened to
me on the way to the grave.

**QUENTIN CRISP**

Probably the toughest time in anyone's life is
when you have to murder a loved one because
they're the devil.

**EMO PHILIPS**

While other people's deaths are deeply sad,
one's own is surely a bit of a joke.

**JAMES CAMERON, *THE OBSERVER*, 1982**

Everything is drive-through. In California they even
have a burial service called Jump-in-the-Box.

**WIL SHRINER**

Making a funny film provides all the enjoyment of getting your leg caught in the blades of a threshing machine. As a matter of fact, it's not even that pleasurable; with the threshing machine the end comes much quicker.

WOODY ALLEN

Now, at last, this sad, glittering century has an image worthy of it: a wandering, wondering girl, a silly Sloane turned secular saint, coming home in a coffin to RAF Northolt like the good soldier she was.

JULIE BURCHILL ON PRINCESS DIANA

Radiation cannot kill you because it contains absolutely no cholesterol.

JOHNNY CARSON

According to most studies, people's number one fear is public speaking. Number two is death. Death is number two. Does that sound right? This means to the average person, if you go to a funeral, you're better off in the casket than doing the eulogy.

JERRY SEINFELD

People are so rude to smokers.
You'd think they'd try to be nicer to people who are dying.

ROSEANNE BARR

■■

The best thing to do, when you've got a dead body
and it's your husband's on the kitchen floor and you
don't know what to do about it, is to make yourself
a good strong cup of tea.

ANTHONY BURGESS

■■

# Some Silly Last Words

If this is justice, I am a banana.

**IAN HISLOP, COMMENTING ON LIBEL DAMAGES THAT *PRIVATE EYE* WAS ORDERED TO PAY SONIA SUTCLIFFE, 1989**

■■

I ask people why they have deer heads on their walls. They always say because it's such a beautiful animal. There you go. I think my mother is attractive, but I have photographs of her.

**ELLEN DEGENERES**

■■

My first part was playing the front end of a horse. He was a serious horse, though.

**SIMON CALLOW**

■■

There's a huge hole in the whole Flood drama, because anything that could float or swim got away scot-free, and it was the idea to wipe out everything, He didn't say, 'I will kill everything, except the floating ones and the swimming ones, who will get out due to a loophole.'

**EDDIE IZZARD ON NOAH'S ARK**

■■

Curiosity killed the cat, but
for a while I was a suspect.

STEVEN WRIGHT

A cement mixer collided with a prison van on the
Kingston Bypass. Motorists are asked to be on
the lookout for sixteen hardened criminals.

RONNIE BARKER AND RONNIE CORBETT

It's amazing that the amount of news that happens in the
world every day always just exactly fits the newspaper.

JERRY SEINFELD

I took a speed-reading course and read *War and
Peace* in twenty minutes. It's about Russia.

WOODY ALLEN

Question: How do you feel about the accident, now you've
had a year to reflect on it?
Answer: I don't sit in trees any more.

KEITH RICHARDS, COMMENTING TO *MOJO* MAGAZINE
ON THE TIME HE FELL OUT OF A COCONUT TREE

I was doing some decorating, so I got out my stepladder.
I don't get on with my real ladder.

**HARRY HILL**

❈

I was walking the streets of Glasgow the other week
and I saw this sign: 'This door is alarmed.'
I said to myself, 'How do you think I feel?'

**ARNOLD BROWN**

❈

My favourite poem is the one that starts 'Thirty days hath
September' because it actually tells you something.

**GROUCHO MARX**

❈

I went to the general store. They wouldn't let
me buy anything specifically.

**STEVEN WRIGHT**

❈

I'm a very good judge of whether
things'll fit through doorways.

**DAVID O'DOHERTY, QUOTED IN
*THE GUARDIAN*, 28 AUGUST 2006**

❈

In the old days, you went from ingénue to old bag,
with a long stretch of unemployment in between.

JULIE WALTERS ON BEING AN ACTOR

■■

I wonder if illiterate people get the full
effect of alphabet soup.

JERRY SEINFELD

■■

The search for the man who terrorizes nudist camps with a
bacon slicer goes on. Inspector Lemuel Jones had a tip-off
this morning, but hopes to be back on duty tomorrow.

RONNIE BARKER AND RONNIE CORBETT

■■

I discovered my wife in bed with another man, and
I was crushed. So I said, 'Get off me, you two.'

EMO PHILIPS

■■

If I were a grouse I'd appeal to the Brace Relations Board.

JILLY COOPER

■■

Is it because I is black?

SASHA BARON COHEN

■■

I asked my teacher what an oxymoron was and he said,
'I don't know what an "oxy" is, bastard.'

**ARTHUR SMITH AND CHRIS ENGLAND**

■■

Wal-mart . . . do they, like, make walls there?

**PARIS HILTON**

■■

What's all this fuss about plutonium? How can something
named after a Disney character be dangerous?

**JOHNNY CARSON**

■■

Some people are always late, like the late King George V.

**SPIKE MILLIGAN**

■■

I'm not a fatalist. But even if I were,
what could I do about it?

**EMO PHILIPS**

■■

A bird in the hand invariably
shits on your wrist.

**BILLY CONNOLLY**

■■

Men's legs have a terribly lonely life –
standing in the dark in your trousers all day.

KEN DODD

Perfume is a subject dear to my heart. I have so many
favourites: Arome de Grenouille, Okéfénôkée, Eau Contraire,
Fume de Ma Tante, Blast du Past, Kèrmes, Je Suis Swell,
and Attention S'il Vous Plaît, to name but a few.

MISS PIGGY, *MISS PIGGY'S GUIDE TO LIFE*

On my first day in New York, a guy asked me if I knew
where Central Park was. When I told him I didn't, he said,
'Do you mind if I mug you here?'

PAUL MERTON

It isn't pollution that's harming the environment.
It's the impurities in our air and water that are doing it.

DAN QUAYLE

I went down the street to the 24-hour grocer. When I got
there, the guy was locking the front. I said, 'Hey, the sign says
you're open 24 hours.' He said, 'Yes, but not in a row.'

STEVEN WRIGHT

I never saw a beggar yet who would recognize
guilt if it bit him on his unwashed ass.

**TONY PARSONS**

When people are on their best behaviour
they aren't always at their best.

**ALAN BENNETT**

To err is human, but to really foul things
up you need a computer.

**PAUL EHRLICH**

Following the dispute with the domestic servants'
union at Buckingham Palace today, the Queen, a radiant
figure in a white silk gown and crimson robe, swept
down the main staircase and through the hall.
She then dusted the cloakroom and vacuumed the lounge.

**RONNIE BARKER AND RONNIE CORBETT,**
***THE TWO RONNIES***

I like a woman with a head on her shoulders.
I hate necks.

**STEVE MARTIN**

# BIBLIOGRAPHY

Amies, Hardy, *The Englishman's Suit* (Quartet Books, 1994)

Beard, Henry, *Miss Piggy's Guide to Life* (Michael Joseph, 1981)

Bennett, Alan, *Enjoy* (Faber & Faber, 1980)

Bennett, Alan, *Habeas Corpus* (Samuel French, 1976)

Bennett, Alan, *Talking Heads* (BBC Books, 2007)

Bennett, Joe, *Fun Run and Other Oxymorons* (Simon & Schuster, 2000)

Bryson, Bill, *A Walk in the Woods* (Black Swan, 1998)

Bryson, Bill, *I'm A Stranger Here Myself: Notes on Returning to America After Twenty Years* (Thorndike Press, 1999)

Bryson, Bill, *Neither Here Nor There: Travels in Europe* (Black Swan, 1998)

Campbell, Alistair, *The Blair Years* (Hutchinson, 2007)

Clarkson, Jeremy, *Born to be Riled: The Collected Writings of Jeremy Clarkson* (BBC Books, 1999)

Cohen, J. M and M. J. (Eds.), *The New Penguin Dictionary of Quotations* (Penguin Books Ltd, 1993)

Cohen, J. M. and M. J. (Eds.), *The Penguin Dictionary of Twentieth-Century Quotations* (Penguin Books Ltd, 1995)

Cohen, J. M. and M. J. (Eds.), *The Penguin Dictionary of Modern Quotations* (Penguin Books Ltd, 1979)

Conran, Shirley, *Superwoman* (Outlet, 1978)

Currie, Edwina, *Diaries 1987–1992* (Time Warner, 2003)

Emin, Tracey, *Strangeland* (Sceptre, 2005)

Ephron, Nora, *Crazy Salad* (Random House, 1975)

Evans, Robert (Ed.), *The Kid Stays in the Picture* (Hyperion, 1992)

Everett, Rupert, *Red Carpets and Other Banana Skins* (Little Brown, 2002)

Fisher, Carrie, *Surrender the Pink* (Vintage, 1991)

French, Marilyn, *The Women's Room* (Virago Press, 1997)

Fry, Stephen, *Paperweight* (Mandarin, 1992)

Goldman, William, *Adventures in the Screen Trade* (Bloomsbury, 1993)

Goldman, William, *Which Lie Did I Tell?* (Bloomsbury, 2000)

Grant, Richard E., *With Nails* (Picador, 1996)

Gray, Simon, *Fat Chance* (Granta Books, 1995)

Heimel, Cynthia, *If You Can't Live Without Me, Why Aren't You Dead Yet?* (Grove/Atlantic, 2002)

Hornby, Nick, *Fever Pitch* (Gollancz, 1992)

Hornby, Nick, *High Fidelity* (Penguin Books Ltd, 2000)

Humphries, Barry, *More Please: An Autobiography* (Viking, 1992)

James, Clive, *Flying Visits* (Jonathan Cape, 1984)

James, Clive, *The Dreaming Swimmer: Non Fiction, 1987–92* (Jonathan Cape, 1992)

Jarski, Rosemarie, *Wrinklies' Wit and Wisdom* (Prion Books Ltd, 2005)

Keillor, Garrison, *The Book of Guys* (Faber & Faber, 1994)

Keyes, Marian, *Last Chance Saloon* (Michael Joseph Ltd, 1999)

King, Billie Jean, *The Autobiography of Billie Jean King* (Granada, 1982)

Klein, Shelley, *The Book of Senior Moments* (Michael O'Mara Books Ltd, 2006)

Knowles, Elizabeth (Ed.), *The Oxford Dictionary of Quotations* (Oxford University Press, 2001)

Leach, Maria, *The Ultimate Insult* (Michael O'Mara Books Ltd, 1996

Lette, Kathy, *Altar Ego* (Picador, 1999)

MacHale, Des (Ed.), *Wit* (Prion Books Ltd, 1997)

Martin, Steve, *Pure Drivel* (Viking, 1999)

Mason, Jackie, *Jackie Mason's America* (Lyle Stuart, 1983)

Mason, Jackie, *The World According to Me* (Simon & Schuster, 1987)

Metcalf, Fred, *The Penguin Dictionary of Modern Humorous Quotations* (Penguin Books Ltd, 2001)

Midler, Bette, *A View from a Broad* (Simon & Schuster, 1980)

Morecambe, Eric and Wise, Ernie, *The Morecambe & Wise Joke Book* (Arthur Barker, 1979)

Muir, Frank and Norden, Denis, *Upon My Word* (Eyre Methuen 1974)

O'Rourke, P. J., *Holidays in Hell* (Picador, 1989)

O'Rourke, P. J., *Modern Manners* (HarperCollins Ltd, 1993)

O'Rourke, P. J., *Parliament of Whores* (Grove/Atlantic, 2003)

Petras, Kathryn and Ross (Ed.), *Age Doesn't Matter Unless You're a Cheese* (Workman Publishing, 2002)

Ratcliffe, Susan, *Oxford Quotations by Subject* (Oxford University Press, 2003)

Sherrin, Ned, *I Wish I'd Said That* (Oxford University Press, 2006)

Spark, Muriel, *Curriculum Vitae: Autobiography* (Constable, 1992)

Tibballs, Geoff (Ed.), *The Mammoth Book of Comic Quotations* (Constable & Robinson Ltd, 2004)

Updike, John, *Picked Up Pieces* (Random House, 1975)

Updike, John, *Problems and Other Stories* (Knopf, 1979)

Weir, Arabella, *Does My Bum Look Big in This?* (Hodder & Stoughton, 1997)

Weisberg, Jacob, *George W. Bushisms* (Fireside, 2001)

Wilkinson, Carl (Ed.), *The Observer Book of Scandal* (Observer Books, 2007)

Young, Toby, *How To Lose Friends and Alienate People* (Abacus, 2001)

# NEWSPAPERS & MAGAZINES

*The Daily Telegraph*

The *Evening Standard*

*The Guardian*

*The Independent*

*The Independent on Sunday*

*The Listener*

*Men's Journal*

*Newsweek*

*The New Yorker*

*The Observer*

*Reader's Digest*

*She*

*The Sunday Telegraph*

*The Sunday Times*

*Time Out*

*Time*

*The Times*

*Today*

# WEBSITES

http://www.aardvarkarchie.com

http://allfunnyquotations.com

http://www.allgreatquotes.com

http://www.amusingquotes.com

http://www.angelfire.com

http://www.basicjokes.com

http://bestfunnyquotes.com

http://www.brainyquote.com

http://www.btinternet.com/
DandyDan/jokes

http://chatna.com

http://www.comedy-zone.net

http://feck.net

http://www.funny.co.uk

http://www.funnyquotes.com

http://geminga.nuigalway.ie

http://www.goodquotes.com

http://www.guy-sports.com/humo

http://www.imdb.com

http://www.innocentenglish.com

http://www.josaka.com

http://www.kitt.net

http://www.lifeisajoke.com

http://monster-island.org

http://politicalhumor.about.com

http://www.saidwhat.co.uk

http://www.some-guy.com

http://www.squidoo.com

http://www.tbns.net

http://www.thinkexist.com

http://www.tinyjo.net/quotes

http://www.quotationspage.com

http://www.whimsical-wits.com

http://www.womansavers.com

http://womenshistory.about.com

http://www.woopidoo.com

http://www.worldofquotes.com

http://www.zaputa.com